INTERNATIONAL STUDENT ENGAGEMENT

INTERNATIONAL STUDENT ENGAGEMENT

Strategies for Creating Inclusive, Connected, and Purposeful Campus Environments

Chris R. Glass, Rachawan Wongtrirat, and Stephanie Buus

Foreword by Fanta Aw

STERLING, VIRGINIA

Published by Stylus Publishing, LLC
22883 Quicksilver Drive
Sterling, Virginia 20166-2102

Library of Congress Cataloging-in-Publication Data
Glass, Chris R.
International student engagement : strategies for creating inclusive,
connected, and purposeful campus environments / Chris R. Glass,
Rachawan Wongtrirat, and Stephanie Buus. -- First Edition.
  pages cm
Includes bibliographical references and index.
ISBN 978-1-62036-147-4 (cloth : alk. paper)
ISBN 978-1-62036-148-1 (pbk. : alk. paper)
ISBN 978-1-62036-149-8 (library networkable e-edition)
ISBN 978-1-62036-150-4 (consumer e-edition)
1. Students, Foreign–United States. 2. College students–United
States. 3. College environment–United States. 4. Student
adjustment--United States. 5. Universities and colleges–United
States–Administration. I. Wongtrirat, Rachawan. II. Buus,
Stephanie. III. Title.
LB2376.4.G53 2015
378.1'982691–dc23

                                                    2014020737

13-digit ISBN: 978-1-62036-147-4 (cloth)
13-digit ISBN: 978-1-62036-148-1 (paperback)
13-digit ISBN: 978-1-62036-149-8 (library networkable e-edition)
13-digit ISBN: 978-1-62036-150-4 (consumer e-edition)

Printed in the United States of America

All first editions printed on acid-free paper
that meets the American National Standards Institute
Z39-48 Standard.

Bulk Purchases

Quantity discounts are available for use in workshops and for
staff development.
Call 1-800-232-0223

First Edition, 2015

For Julie Sinclair, Chalintorn Burian, Dana Burnett, and Regina Karp,
whose dedication to international students inspires us

CONTENTS

FOREWORD

Close to three decades ago, I came to the United States in pursuit of an education. I found my voice and my home at American University in Washington, D.C., owing largely to an environment that embraced a culture of inclusivity, cross-cultural engagement, and student-leadership development. I have argued that those years as an international student in the United States were transformative: they led to my career as an international educator and inspired me to engage in a leadership role in the field. It is my hope that the extraordinary education and engagement I was afforded as an international student so long ago is one that can be experienced by every international student who chooses to study in the United States. However, I have learned from experience—over more than two decades as a scholar and practitioner in international education—that while far too many institutions in the United States strive to internationalize their campuses, their rhetoric often does not match the reality on the ground. Too many institutions struggle to effectively integrate international students and leverage their knowledge and experiences to advance cross-cultural understanding and educational exchange for both international and domestic students.

International Student Engagement: Strategies for Creating Inclusive, Connected, and Purposeful Campus Environments is the first of its kind to provide a holistic approach to the important and timely subject of inclusion and integration of international students and the structural forces at play. The authors draw from first-person narratives, case examples of effective institutional practices and policies, and curricular and cocurricular initiatives to illustrate the myriad ways to effectively engage international students and to transform educational environments. The book gives voice to the international student experience and provides tangible and concrete examples of effective practices. At a time when the number of international students is growing—in large part due to increased international recruitment practices and institutions' need to advance educational, economic, and social imperatives—it is crucial that as international educators we heed the call to ensure that every international student is afforded a rich educational experience in and out of the classroom, and that high impact programs become the norm rather than the exception. Glass, Wongtrirat, and Buus remind us of our commitment to international students and provide much needed resources for ensuring robust engagement of students. The authors of this book should be applauded for their vision, foresight, and contributions to the field.

Every practitioner working with international students and committed to enhancing the student experience should read this book.

Fanta Aw
Hust Senior Professorial Lecturer, School of International
Service, American University;
President and Chair of the Board of Directors,
NAFSA: Association of International Educators;
Assistant Vice President of Campus Life, American University

INTRODUCTION
Strengthening Campus Commitments to International Students

Over the last two decades, American higher education has transitioned from an arena of elite mobility to mass global student mobility. Each day, almost 1 million international students make their way to class at U.S. higher education institutions, ranging from community colleges in small rural towns to elite private universities in some of America's largest cities (Institute of International Education [IIE], 2013). International students participate in campus organizations, eat dorm food, call home, and relax with friends. They interact with faculty, staff, and students who affect their developmental trajectories in ways both large and small. And they form relationships with these groups, some that last over time and space and some that are more casual and immediate. In 1950, just over 25,000 international students studied in the United States. A little over 15 years later, enrollment surpassed the 100,000 mark; by the turn of the century, enrollment reached a half million students. In the last decade, international student enrollment has almost doubled, from 514,723 in 1999–2000 to 819,644 in 2012–2013, and it is now poised to surpass the 1 million mark (IIE, 2013).

Just as the move from elite to mass higher education transformed the American higher education system after World War II, the rise of mass global student mobility has the potential to significantly reshape American higher education in the coming decades. The presence of international students at U.S. colleges and universities is nothing new. What has changed is the size and scope of international student recruitment efforts (Adams, Leventhal, & Connelly, 2012). Over half of U.S. colleges and universities surveyed by IIE in 2013 reported that their institutions now had a growing reputation abroad. A statement from University of South Florida's vice provost for international initiatives summed up both the size and scope of the explosion of international student enrollment: "We are now known in places that ten years ago had never heard of us" (Hayes, 2013, para. 10).

As international recruitment has become central to academic planning and university budgets (Adams, Leventhal, & Connelly, 2012;

1

Choudaha, 2012), the profile of international students has diversified and changed significantly in the past decade (Choudaha, Orosz, & Chang, 2012). This shift in the profile of international students enrolling in U.S. colleges and universities has in turn challenged common assumptions about student learning and development (Lee, 2013). Moreover, making campus internationalization work so that international students become integral to campus life is easier said than done. Institutional strategic plans assert that "international students add diversity to a mostly homogenous campus" and that studying in the United States is "a great educational opportunity for these students" (Porter & Belkin, 2013, para. 6). However, current evidence that cultural diversity, in the form of increased international student enrollments, contributes to the development of intercultural learning among U.S. students is relatively thin (see Deardorff & Jones, 2012; Leask, 2009; Wächter, 2003).

International student enrollments often expand without sufficient consideration of how these enrollments will affect the campus culture(s) already in place and which capacities will be required to create a campus climate capable of including new and diverse populations. Instead, the rhetoric adopted by universities cheerfully suggests that it is possible to have "'diversity' without conflict" (Graff, 1994, p. 28; Lambert & Usher, 2013). Accordingly, international enrollments may go forward with little attention paid to the actual readiness of domestic students to create a tolerant and welcoming context for incoming international students. At the same time, a spate of recent cases at U.S. universities and colleges illustrates the deleterious, and even tragic, effects that the unfettered and aimless enrollment of large numbers of international students can have on their well-being once they arrive on campus, including depression, loneliness, and isolation (Fischer, 2012; Gareis, 2012; Glass & Braskamp, 2012; Redden, 2012; Sawir, Marginson, Deumert, Nyland, & Ramia, 2007). For example, a Nepalese student wrote an op-ed about her experience living alone "in a dreary box room" for two years as she struggled to study and meet her financial obligations. She asks, "Universities are eager to accept our fees—but are they doing enough to support young people like me who come from far away to study?" (Paudel, 2013).

Not surprisingly, then, international educators, activists, and journalists are increasingly calling for closer attention to the qualitative dimensions of international students' experiences at U.S. colleges and universities (Fischer, 2014; Lee, 2014). International educators work tirelessly, often on limited budgets, to engage international students directly and to push for more inclusive campus environments for these students. Many international educators enter the field for humanitarian or social justice reasons with an eye on the potential benefits of enhanced intercultural understanding. Academic exchange has long been a core feature of cultural diplomacy, and increased educational exchange holds great potential as a force for enhancing intercultural understanding and promoting international development. In this vein, international students are often approached as a resource for diversifying student populations and as an aid for U.S. students interested in strengthening their ability to navigate cultural differences in a global society and marketplace (Jayakumar, 2008).

An international student enrollment survey conducted by IIE in 2012 found that almost 60% of U.S. institutions reported an increase in international student enrollments for that year. International student enrollments have climbed for seven straight years (2006–2012), and the figures continue to escalate. Of those institutions with more than 1,000 international students, 80% reported increases. Forty percent more international students enroll at U.S. colleges and universities than did 10 years ago. Among U.S. baccalaureate institutions, one in five reported substantial increases in the number of international students enrolled. In turn, 70% of institutions reported that they had taken action to ensure that international student enrollments would not decline, including hiring new staff, reallocating the duties of existing staff to cover international enrollments, and forming new partnerships and forms of collaboration abroad. Most of the top-20 U.S. institutions hosting international students reported modest increases in international enrollments, which suggests that those institutions with traditionally smaller enrollments—and likely few established programs for incoming international students—have seen the most substantial increases. Such institutions have seen their enrollments skyrocket, doubling or even tripling within the course of a year or two.

Weaving Together the Big and Small Stories

In this book, we outline deep approaches to the academic and social integration of international students at U.S. colleges and universities. We describe concrete examples of strategies to enhance the international student experience across a wide range of institutional types (e.g., community colleges, liberal arts colleges, and research universities). The book explores actions that have enabled colleges and universities to create more inclusive, connected, and purposeful campus environments for international students. It fleshes out the effects of these actions through the first-person narratives of international students themselves. The focus of this book, then, is on reinforcing an institution's existing strengths and capacities to help academic leaders develop comprehensive strategies that will enable the creation of inclusive campus climates for international students.

To achieve this ambitious goal, we attempt to weave together the "big stories" of how institutions are strengthening and deepening their campus commitment to international students with the "small stories," the first-person-narrative experiences, of the international students we interviewed in our research. We connect the big stories of the Global Perspective Inventory (GPI) data set with the small stories of the meaning of these developmentally effective experiences in the lives of international students. We tell the two stories in parallel to illustrate how the small stories of students and the big stories institutions intersect and cocreate one another. Without keeping both narratives in view, the big stories can be lost in abstraction and remain distant from the real-life consequences of institutional policies, practice, and programs; and the small stories leave us inspired or pained without concrete examples of policies, programs, and practices to learn from and adapt in order to enhance the international student experience.

Amplifying Student Voices

I can see from semester to semester how I grow intellectually and how I am able to do much more than I thought I would ever be able to do. The educational system here, I think, or this particular program and the people I'm surrounded by, kind of made me realize how people have so much potential but maybe they never actually try to use it or develop it. I have a feeling with this program I'll always need to actually develop my potential and see what I can actually do. It's just amazing! (Graduate, female from Eastern Europe)

When I look back, I think I have grown in that I thought I was a pretty open-minded person, but after coming here and meeting all [the] people, I became more open-minded in that sense like trying to understand other people from where they come from rather than just assuming my own ideas. When I just came in, I didn't expect that to happen. I thought I'll just come in, go to classes, get my degree, and be done with it, and people like—maybe I'll talk with people from [my country] and I'll just be done with it. The expectation was nothing at all like nothing in terms of growth, except academic. Maybe I thought I might be a little bit independent because I'll be living on my own but that's about it. (Graduate, female from Southern Asia)

These international students are flourishing. They describe engaging in meaningful experiences, a sense of meaning and purpose, supportive relationships, emotional well-being, and a sense of confidence and achievement during college.

One of the primary goals of this book is to amplify the voices of international students in the process of campus internationalization. Hearing student voices firsthand offers the reader a rare opportunity to understand the international student experience from the inside. Stories and firsthand accounts provide a concreteness and refreshing perspective that large-scale national surveys miss. Personal narratives also show that not all experiences affect international students equally. A racist encounter can be debilitating for one student and may strengthen a sense of resolve and ethnic identity for another. Moreover, various combinations of experiences—not just a single best practice—contribute to students' development. By listening, we have a lot to learn, and they have much to say. Like Walt Whitman (1892) in his poem "Song of Myself," international students do not speak with a single voice or single view. In Whitman's words, they "contain multitudes." The stories we share invite the reader to see the resilience, activism, courage, and experiences that are developmentally significant in shifting the students' perspectives both on life in the United States and on themselves.

The rich narratives included in this book reflect Gargano's (2009) assertion that scholars should "place student voices at the forefront of a discourse on student mobility" (p. 343). Consequently, this book not only describes concrete examples of policies, programs, and practices that colleges and universities can learn from and adapt to enhance the international student experience, but it is also filled with the voices of international students. We draw on 40 in-depth interviews with international students sharing success as well as difficulties and struggles navigating college life in the United States. Narratives like those in this book allow us to enter into the international students' experiences, drawing on their courage and identifying with the complex and intense interactions that shape them.

Cross-Campus Connections

One of the aims of this book is to take readers on a journey, from community colleges to liberal arts institutions to large public flagship research universities, from rural parts of the United States to highly populated urban areas. Our goal is to raise questions that provoke the reader to think about how university life has changed with the surge of international students and the challenges that confront senior administrators seeking to strengthen and deepen connections for the students.

We set out to identify colleges and universities that are strengthening their commitments to international students in three important areas: strengthening connections among various units, exploring ways to deepen the quality of the international student experience, and expanding the number of students engaged in international, global, and intercultural learning. We used the GPI and our relationships with over 135 colleges to identify institutions that are demonstrating promising practices that are enhancing the international student experience.

The institutions vary in size, location, educational mission, and composition of international students yet share a commitment to comprehensive internationalization and take seriously the concrete practices that create developmentally effective environments for international students. They do not leave the international student experience to chance; each institution has taken into consideration the changing demographics of international students as they develop programs, policies, and practices that create positive campus climates for these students. They have made practical decisions to devote human resources, time, and money to initiatives that foster the success of international students.

The institutions in this book are just a handful of a larger number of institutions that are doing excellent work in the areas we highlight. Since the engagement of international students will vary from campus to campus, we did not set out to select "the most successful" institutions; we did highlight practices that we thought other institutions could adapt to their own context. Solutions are contextual, so our emphasis is on the key features of educational experiences that create positive campus environments for international students. Since the institutions we highlight in this book represent a diversity of histories, missions, and initiatives, we begin by providing a brief background of each institution before jumping into in-depth examination of specific contexts and arenas these institutions are working in to enhance the international student experience.

Elon University

Elon University's pastoral campus located in the Piedmont region of North Carolina brings worlds together. This intimate, closely connected campus community is a short drive away from one of North Carolina's largest cities, Greensboro. Elon is best known for its rags-to-riches story of institutional transformation, which took place in the 1970s, when Elon catapulted itself from obscurity to a selective, nationally recognized university known for exemplary study abroad programs, among other distinctions. Elon consistently ranks in the top 10% on the key benchmarks of the National Survey of Student Engagement (NSSE), and it is a renowned national model of excellence in engaged learning. This independent, private liberal arts university was originally named Elon College. In 2001, after its transformation and the creation of robust professional programs, it changed its name to Elon University. The university infuses its mission throughout the student experience, embracing the founders' vision of "an academic community that transforms mind, body, and spirit and encourages freedom of thought and liberty of conscience" (Elon University, n.d.). To accomplish its mission, Elon focuses on active student engagement with faculty, a dynamic liberal arts and sciences curriculum, integration of knowledge across fields and disciplines, and a fundamental respect for human diversity. In 2012, 72% of students attending Elon had a study abroad experience. Many institutions would view that level of participation as phenomenal success given that national averages for study abroad participation hover around 3% and in North Carolina the percentage of students studying abroad is less than 2% (National Association of Foreign Student Advisers [NAFSA], 2011).

The administrators leading internationalization efforts looked at those numbers and asked themselves, "How can we allow even more students to engage in a cross-cultural experience?" International students enrolled at Elon mostly come from large, urban cities and discover the beautiful, rural countryside of North Carolina's Piedmont. Phil Smith, director of the Study USA program at Elon, asked his colleagues, "What can we do to have international students experience more while they are here, to deepen and make their experience richer?" International students coming from large cities abroad now enhance their global experience with study away experiences in places from New York City to a small coal-mining town in Kentucky. Study away programs allow students with diverse perspectives to engage in what Elon describes as a "global experience"—purposefully designed experiences in which students encounter people different from themselves. Chapter 3 highlights how Elon is seeking to leverage "encounters with difference that make a difference" through its Study USA program.

Florida International University

Florida International University (FIU), a top-tier, student-centered, public research university, prizes its commitment to being "worlds ahead in its service to the academic and local community." The word *international* is not just central to the name of this institution; FIU has infused global learning throughout its undergraduate curriculum. A 2013 article in *Inside Higher Ed* described the curriculum as putting "the 'I' in FIU" (Redden, 2013). Founded only 50 years ago, FIU has distinguished itself as one of the most competitive universities in the state in terms of admissions. Woven into the heart of Miami, FIU's 344-acre campus was built at the site of a local airfield. Today, FIU is a destination for globally mobile students.

Its lush, green campus complex is a vibrant habitat for creativity and innovation that prepares graduates to "succeed in a global market." FIU is a place where the traditional definition of *international students* as those "who travel to a country different from their own for the purpose of tertiary study" (Organisation for Economic Co-operation and Development, 2003, para. 1) is too narrow. A broader definition that includes first- and second-generation Americans reveals the diversity of students who call FIU their alma mater, since the institution serves a large number of Spanish-speaking Americans who grew up in Miami but whose parents came from South or Central America.

International students from China, Venezuela, India, Saudi Arabia, and Colombia intermix with FIU's large Hispanic population. Of the over 50,000 students who attend FIU, more than 85% are considered minorities. The university's mission zeroes in on its diversity: "Florida International University is an urban, multi-campus, public research university serving its students and a diverse population of South Florida. We are committed to high quality teaching, state-of-the-art research and creative activity, and collaborative engagement with our local and global communities" (FIU, 2013).

Hilary Landorf, director of global learning initiatives, leads FIU's quality enhancement plan (QEP), Global Learning for Global Citizenship. This university-wide initiative includes a graduation requirement for all undergraduates of a minimum of two classes that are infused with global learning outcomes. These courses, as Landorf puts it, enable students to "view the world from multiple perspectives, attain knowledge of global interconnections, and graduate from the university willing to address local and global issues through critical thinking and problem solving." Initiatives designed to enhance the international student experience often myopically focus on international student programming. In contrast, the comprehensive approach at FIU is aimed at creating a social environment and positive campus climate to enhance intercultural understanding for all students. Florida International University is strengthening and deepening its commitment to international students by ensuring that international students—in the broadest sense of the word—engage deeply in experiences so they graduate as "responsible global citizens." Chapter 1 highlights the key factors that helped FIU internationalize its curriculum.

Indiana University–Bloomington

In 1909 the U.S. Bureau of Education conducted its first Foreign Student Services Survey to assess how higher education was serving Chinese students. A questionnaire was sent to 100 institutions asking about facilities, number of students, scholarships, and services. Indiana University–Bloomington (IU) responded to the questionnaire, reporting one Chinese student, living in a private home off-campus and paying $40 in tuition each year.

A hundred years later, IU was one of the top 25 institutions hosting international students, home to a bustling 6,123 foreign-born students (IIE, 2012). Christopher Viers, the associate vice president for international services at IU, is facilitating opportunities for international and domestic students to build relationships. IU has purposely sought to move beyond the "one time annual event" and encourage cross-cultural interaction at a more micro-level. International students consistently rate informal interactions with their U.S. peers as some of the most meaningful and important learning experiences. Viers originally was a pre-med major with plans to work as an emergency room physician. His own cross-cultural encounters during college with people from other countries and cultures expanded his view of the world and created in him a passion for international education. Now, having seen the transformative potential of cross-cultural interaction, Viers is an ardent advocate who helps students at IU

> see the world through the eyes of international students as I had come to do. I strive to find ways for others to know the caliber of the students, their reasons for study in the U.S., the sacrifices they make in pursuing U.S. higher education, and their seriousness of purpose. Fear keeps so many people from that experience. ("Serving International Students," 2009, p. 19)

Bloomington, Indiana, is a "quintessential college town" with a population of 70,000 people, almost 60% of whom are graduate or undergraduate students. The university strives to provide the "ideal college experience," attracting students from around the world with its "great traditions, gorgeous campus, international culture, Big Ten sports, and active academic climate" (IU, 2013, para. 1). As the flagship institution of the IU campus system, Bloomington is committed to the mission that provides "broad access to undergraduate, graduate, and continuing education for students throughout Indiana, the U.S., and the world, as well as outstanding academic and cultural programs and student services" (IU, 2014, para. 1).

Keeping track of over 6,000 international students has led to university-wide efforts to create sunapsis, a proactive case management and tracking system that ensures the university is engaging international students before issues and problems arise with visa issues or student academic performance. This proactive, data-driven, evidence-based approach to enhance the international student experience demonstrates a concrete commitment by senior administrators to enhance the campus climate for international students and support their student success. Chapter 4 highlights how IU is taking a data-driven approach to enhancing international student success.

Northern Arizona University

Northern Arizona University (NAU) touts that it

> opened its doors in 1899 with 23 students, one professor, and two copies of Webster's International Dictionary bound in sheepskin. The first president scoured the countryside in a horse and buggy seeking students to fill the classrooms of a single school building. (NAU, 2014, para. 1)

Today, NAU is home to 26,000 students and 900 full-time faculty. It has experienced eight straight years of international student enrollment growth. Over 1,000 international students, double the number from just five years ago, from 60 countries call NAU their home.

As an institution, NAU has challenged the notion that internationalization is a luxury that cannot be afforded. "The exact opposite is true," according to Harvey Charles, vice provost for international education at the university. "A well-resourced internationalization infrastructure means that there are resources to fund global learning projects and other university priorities" (as cited in Redden, 2013, 'Comprehensive Internationalization,' para. 2). Rather than focusing on the obstacles to achieving comprehensive internationalization, NAU has emphasized how investing in comprehensive internationalization efforts generates more resources to fulfill the academic mission of the institution. It has championed an approach to budget and planning that reinvests revenue from expanded international elements into strengthening and deepening campus internationalization efforts. NAU, winner of the Senator Paul Simon Award for Comprehensive Internationalization in 2012, has demonstrated its dedication to deepening and strengthening its commitments to international students.

NAU acknowledges the integral role that housing and residence life play by providing and creating a home for international students. It values the contribution that a robust international community makes to academic initiatives that span the globe, such as science, engineering, technology, and mathematics programs. Located in Flagstaff, Arizona, near Grand Canyon National Park, NAU sees the important cultural role in forging strong connections between the global community and the local public. Among its initiatives, NAU is investing in the concrete features of the student experience, especially in areas of housing and residence life. International houses have a long and storied tradition in international education. Chapter 4 explores the new international house (I-House) at NAU.

Old Dominion University

Old Dominion University (ODU) prides itself on being a vibrant, metropolitan university at the commercial and cultural crossroads of southern

Virginia. Partnership is part and parcel of the culture of this vibrant research university. The campus ethos exemplifies "idea fusion," the cross-disciplinary partnering of top researchers with an extensive range of businesses, community organizations, and the greater metropolitan region of Hampton Roads. Located just a few miles from the Port of Virginia, the deepest shipping channel on the U.S. East Coast, ODU has a prominent role in international affairs and the economy of the Commonwealth of Virginia. Undergraduates learn to live, study, and work on a multicultural campus in one of the most culturally diverse regions of Virginia. ODU is among the most ethnically diverse institutions in Virginia; one-third of every freshman class is composed of Filipino, Asian, African American, and Hispanic students. The university's modern buildings and entrepreneurial approach to problem solving has attracted over 1,400 international students—about 6% of its student population—from more than 110 nations around the world.

ODU has made it a strategic priority to create a coordinated service model for international students and scholars and to implement curricular and cocurricular programs that develop culturally competent students. It has made support for international students and their families a strategic priority, including multiple initiatives designed to assist with cultural orientation, housing, health care, family support, child care, and mentoring. Moreover, campus leaders strive to invest strategically in avenues that nurture continued ties with international alumni after they graduate. The university's original motto, "A Portal to New Worlds," reflects a fundamental commitment of campus educators to integrate the diverse cultural traditions represented at ODU throughout campus life. Spearheading these efforts is the Office of Intercultural Relations (OIR), with a mandate to "cultivate a climate of understanding and respect that yields authentic interactions with diverse individuals and groups" (OIR, 2014, para. 1). Old Dominion University has distinguished itself not just as a provider of student services, but as an organizer of an active and engaged International Student Advisory Board (ISAB), willing to advocate for issues on behalf of its international student population. Chapter 2 describes the formation and evolution of the ISAB at ODU.

Valencia College

Valencia College awards more associate degrees than any other two-year school in the United States ("Valencia No. 1," 2010), and almost 40% of those degrees are awarded to minority students. When the campus opened in 1967, it served a predominantly White student population; today, the campus is very multicultural. Diversity is the norm; students are used to being surrounded by people from other places, according to Jennifer Robertson, director of study abroad and global experiences at Valencia. Robertson cited a recent campus survey in which 97% of students said they felt comfortable interacting across cultures. Students date across cultures. They seek roommates across cultures.

Founded as a community college, the institution has dramatically expanded its academic scope in the last 50 years. Today, the college extends to five campuses in Orange and Osceola Counties in Central Florida. The entrepreneurial spirit of Valencia spawned numerous innovative international initiatives over the years. The first, started in 2001, was the nondegree Intensive English Program, which has seen tremendous success in international student recruitment over the last decade, and in 2006 the college established the Study Abroad and Global Experiences Office to coordinate outbound study abroad initiatives. One of the boldest moves was transferring International Student Services to the Continuing Education division, which already had a well-established international student recruitment process in place. To coordinate these efforts in an educationally purposeful way, Valencia committed itself to strengthening the connections among the initiatives by breaking down the silos and fostering a culture of collaboration for all aspects of internationalization. Today, with a greater strategic focus, Valencia is on the brink of creating a culture in which faculty administrators and staff work together across the college to connect the different international initiatives. Recruitment, admissions, academic advising, immigration advising, programming, and counseling for international students are all under the umbrella of International Student Services.

Strengthening these connections became an opportunity for Valencia to continue to invigorate a culture of excellence, reinforce its identity as an international campus, and deepen the quality of the various international initiatives. Internationalization is a hallmark of the campus effort to "provide opportunities for academic, technical and lifelong learning in a collaborative culture dedicated to inquiry, results, and excellence," according to Robertson. The college prides itself on helping students achieve more than they dreamed would be possible, and it has been nationally recognized for its "innovative thinking and laser-focused commitment to student success," receiving the inaugural Aspen Prize for Community College Excellence (Dembicki, 2011, para. 4). The college has organized itself to be even more integrated in order to direct that same laser-like focus on supporting the international students seeking two-year and four-year degrees. It has taken a comprehensive approach to internationalization by increasing academic exchanges and international student enrollment, expanding study abroad opportunities, and infusing global and intercultural learning throughout the curriculum. The reorganization transformed its siloed approach to one offering comprehensive services to international students.

International students have been a priority at Valencia for a long time. A new culture has taken hold—one that sees shared purposes between its traditional, regionally focused economic and strategic initiatives and its expanding global connections. Robertson described this holistic approach to internationalization as a "new culture of embracing international students, and bringing them into the college, seeing them not just as a source of revenue, but also how they can enhance the environment of the college as well."

Top sending countries include Venezuela, Brazil, Saudi Arabia, and China. In addition, because of geographic proximity, a significant percentage of international students come from countries in the Caribbean Basin, such Haiti, Bahamas, and Jamaica. Valencia has a highly diverse international student population with students from over 80 countries; this diversity is increasingly becoming an interconnected part of Valencia's identity. Chapter 2 highlights how Valencia is connecting international students with its campus and local community.

Valparaiso University

Just an hour southeast of Chicago, Valparaiso University is the largest independent Lutheran university in the United States. The curriculum at Valpo, as the university is sometimes called, is rooted in liberal arts tradition and maintains a highly residential ethos characterized by strong and supportive relationships among faculty and students. Over two-thirds of students arrive from out of state and nearly 50 countries around the world. The university believes "now is the best time to start preparing for a future in this interconnected world" (Valparaiso University, n.d.-a, para. 2). The faculty and staff at Valpo live out its mission to be "a community of learning dedicated to excellence and grounded in the Lutheran tradition of scholarship, freedom, and faith, [which] prepares students to lead and serve in both church and society." Reflecting the institution's core commitments to liberal learning, Valpo has numerous study abroad programs and an on-campus learning environment that leverages diversity to engage students with the diverse cultural and religious traditions of the world. As a faith-based institution, Valpo makes its commitment to the "creative relationship between faith and learning" (Valparaiso University, n.d.-b, para.1) by attending to the interior lives of students, exploring questions of value, identity, ethics, and meaning.

Valpo has been recruiting foreign students throughout its 125-year history. Ten years ago, the percentage of international students reflected the national average: around 4% of the total student population (C. Schaefer, personal communication, July 22, 2013). In the next 10 years, Valpo, like many institutions around the United States, expects over 15% of its student population, or nearly 600 students, to be foreign-born (Valparaiso

University, 2013). Chuck Schaefer, chair of the International Studies Department, characterized current enrollment trends as "exponential growth." As is the case in many U.S. institutions, a large proportion of the international enrollment growth comes from an influx of Chinese students from middle-class families. Valpo hosts the first Confucius Institute of any small, church-based institution in the United States and has developed a close academic exchange partnership with Zhejiang University in Hangzhou, China. Valpo also hosts over 160 students from the Middle East, including Saudi Arabia, Iraq, Kuwait, and the United Arab Emirates. Strong partnerships that promote scholarly exchange of faculty have paved the road for sustainable, mutually beneficial partnerships. Schaefer believes the challenges of such a large influx of students do not fit easily into a paradigm in which international students just "acculturate to the U.S." The new generation of international students, from his perspective, require international educators to view today's globally mobile students as a more cosmopolitan-minded population: "The attraction is to become part of a globalized transnational ex-patriot group of people who have more in common with one another than they often times do with their own nationals." Chapter 1 highlights how Valpo is investing in faculty learning and professional growth.

Organization of Each Chapter

A comprehensive resource for international educators, faculty, and student affairs staff, this book describes the social contexts that contribute to enhancing the international student experience and outlines deep approaches to the academic and social integration of international students at U.S. colleges and universities. Each chapter consists of four key, integrated elements:

1. A discussion of contemporary issues and trends from research literature and the popular press
2. Research from the GPI that identifies and describes high-impact curricular and cocurricular experiences
3. The first-person narratives of international students themselves
4. Campus-level case examples of policies, programs, and practices that other colleges and universities can adapt to their own campus context to better meet the complex needs of international students

Chapter 1 examines curricular experiences that contribute to cross-cultural interaction and an enhanced sense of belonging for international students. The student narratives reveal the role that intergroup dialogue and faculty–student interactions play in building international students' sense of belonging. We use both narratives and institutional examples to demonstrate in a more holistic way the critical role that faculty members play in the social and academic integration of international students.

Chapter 2 describes cocurricular experiences that contribute to cross-cultural interaction and an enhanced sense of belonging among international students. Student narratives in turn confirm the importance of student engagement and leadership programs that enhance a sense of belonging for international students.

Chapter 3 describes the role of friendship networks in international students' well-being and academic success. Student narratives highlight qualitative aspects of students' relationships that contribute to their sense of belonging.

Chapter 4 describes how relationships with family members affect international students' sense of belonging. Student narratives describe how students manage family obligations and negotiate tensions among individual, familial, and other collective needs, desires, and goals. This chapter also discusses how use of social media with home- and host-country peers affects international students' sense of belonging. Student narratives describe a widespread, but little-discussed, problem of discrimination against international students in online environments: students face more blatant discrimination off campus than on, including through social media.

Chapter 5 revisits one of the core themes of this book: enhancing international students' sense of belonging. We suggest three subtle but important ways that international educators and administrators might expand the ways we approach the issue of belonging when it comes to the international student population at U.S. colleges and universities. This chapter builds on core themes in the book and highlights the role of belonging in terms of student academic engagement and success. We will show that belonging in all of its forms—resilience building, engagement and deliberative democratic discussion, and diversified student social networks—are critical elements as well as outcomes of the classroom experience.

Chapter 6 offers recommendations for colleges and universities that are committed to enhancing the international student experience. We believe that deep and meaningful change can be accomplished not by one office, but rather through collaborations among departments and offices across campus and the community—most importantly, the international student community.

References

Adams, T., Leventhal, M., & Connelly, S. (2012). International student recruitment in Australia and the United States: Approaches and attitudes. In D. K. Deardorff, H. de Wit, J. D. Heyl, & T. Adams (Eds.), *The SAGE handbook of international higher education* (pp. 399–416). New York, NY: SAGE Publications.

Choudaha, R. (2012, December 13). Foreign students becoming integral to budgets of universities [Web log post]. *DrEducation: International Higher Education Blog.* Retrieved from http://www.dreducation.com/2012/12/public-university-foreign-student-economic.html

Choudaha, R., Orosz, K., & Chang, L. (2012). *Not all international students are the same: Understanding segments, mapping behavior.* New York, NY: World Education Services.

Deardorff, D. K., & Jones, E. (2012). Intercultural competence: An emerging focus in international higher education. In D. K. Deardorff, H. de Wit, J. D. Heyl, & T. Adams (Eds.), *The SAGE handbook of international higher education* (pp. 283–303). New York, NY: SAGE Publications.

Dembicki, M. (2011, December 12). Valencia College receives Aspen Prize. *Community College Daily.* Retrieved from http://www.ccdaily.com/Pages/Campus-Issues/Valencia-College-receives-Aspen-Prize.aspx

Elon University. (n.d.). *About Elon University.* Retrieved March 1, 2014, from http://www.elon.edu/e-web/about/default.xhtml

Fischer, K. (2012, June 14). Many foreign students are friendless in the U.S., study finds. *Chronicle of Higher Education.* Retrieved from http://chronicle.com/article/Many-Foreign-Students-Find/132275/

Fischer, K. (2014, March 2). Helping foreign students thrive on U.S. campuses. *New York Times.* Retrieved from http://www.nytimes.com/2014/03/03/world/americas/helping-foreign-students-thrive-on-us-campuses.html

Florida International University. (2013). *Vision and mission.* Retrieved from http://www.fiu.edu/about-us/vision-mission/index.html

Gareis, E. (2012). Intercultural friendship: Effects of home and host region. *Journal of International and Intercultural Communication, 5*(4), 1–20. doi:10.1080/17513057.2012.691525

Gargano, T. (2009). (Re)conceptualizing international student mobility: The potential of transnational social fields. *Journal of Studies in International Education, 13*(3), 331–346. doi:10.1177/1028315308322060

Glass, C. R., & Braskamp, L. A. (2012, October 26). Foreign students and tolerance. *Inside Higher Ed.* Retrieved from http://www.insidehighered.com/views/2012/10/26/essay-how-colleges-should-respond-racism-against-international-students

Graff, G. (1994). Other voices, other rooms: Organizing and teaching the humanities conflict. In W. E. Cain (Ed.), *Teaching the conflicts* (pp. 17–44). New York, NY: Garland Publishing.

Hayes, S. (2013, October 5). At USF, international students bring diversity and dollars. *Tampa Bay Times.* Retrieved from http://www.tampabay.com/news/education/college/at-usf-international-students-bring-diversity-and-dollars/2145750

Indiana University. (2013). *Life in Bloomington.* Retrieved from http://music .indiana.edu/about/bloomington/index.shtml

Indiana University. (2014). *Mission.* Retrieved from http://www.indiana.edu/about/ mission.shtml

Institute of International Education. (2012). *Fall 2012 international student enrollment survey.* Washington, DC: Author.

Institute of International Education. (2013). *Open Doors 2013 report on international educational exchange.* Washington, DC: Author.

Jayakumar, U. (2008). Can higher education meet the needs of an increasingly diverse and global society? Campus diversity and cross-cultural workforce competencies. *Harvard Educational Review, 78*(4), 615–651.

Lambert, J., & Usher, A. (2013). *Internationalization and the domestic student experience.* Toronto, ON: Higher Education Strategy Associates.

Leask, B. (2009). Using formal and informal curricula to improve interactions between home and international students. *Journal of Studies in International Education, 13*(2), 205–221. doi:10.1177/1028315308329786

Lee, J. J. (2013). *Discussant comments in the Perceptions and Experiences of International Students in Higher Education.* San Francisco, CA: American Educational Research Association.

Lee, J. J. (2014). Internationalization as acquisitions, mergers, and synergy: A value-based framework of internationalization. *IIE Networker, 37*, 25–27.

National Association of Foreign Student Advisers. (2011). *Study abroad participation by state: Academic year 2010–2011.* Retrieved from http://www.nafsa.org/ uploadedFiles/Chez_NAFSA/Explore_International_Education/Impact/Data_ And_Statistics/state by state 10_11 study abroad statistics.pdf

Northern Arizona University. (2014). *History.* Retrieved from http://nau.edu/About/ Who-We-Are/History/

Office of Intercultural Relations, Old Dominion University. (2014). *Mission.* Retrieved from http://www.odu.edu/oir

Organisation for Economic Co-operation and Development. (2003, March 5). Foreign students. *Glossary of statistical terms.* Retrieved from http://stats.oecd.org/ glossary/detail.asp?ID=1052

Paudel, S. (2013, September 12). Poor, isolated, and far from home: What it's like to be an international student. *Guardian.* Retrieved from http://www.theguardian .com/education/mortarboard/2013/sep/12/what-its-like-to-be-an-international -student

Porter, C., & Belkin, D. (2013, November 11). Record number of foreign students flocking to U.S. *Wall Street Journal.* Retrieved from http://online.wsj.com/news/ articles/SB10001424052702304868404579190062164404756

Redden, E. (2012, October 16). I'm not racist, but. *Inside Higher Ed.* Retrieved http://www.insidehighered.com/news/2012/10/16/tensions-simmer-between -american-and-international-students

Redden, E. (2013, October 7). Grappling with global learning. *Inside Higher Ed.* Retrieved from http://www.insidehighered.com/news/2013/10/07/conference -focuses-integrating-global-learning-within-curriculum

Sawir, E., Marginson, S., Deumert, A., Nyland, C., & Ramia, G. (2007). Loneliness and international students: An Australian study. *Journal of Studies in International Education, 12*(2), 148–180. doi:10.1177/1028315307299699

Serving international students and scholars. (2009, Spring). *IU International Magazine.* Retrieved from http://worldwide.iu.edu/communications/magazine/issues/2009/spring/articles/serving.pdf

Valencia No.1 for associate degrees. (2010, June 18). *Orlando Business Journal.* Retrieved from http://www.bizjournals.com/orlando/stories/2010/06/14/daily53.html

Valparaiso University. (2013, September 11). Valparaiso University named top university by *U.S. News* for 25 consecutive years. *Valpo Today.* Retrieved from http://www.valpo.edu/news/2013/09/11/valparaiso-university-named-top-university-by-u-s-news-for-25-consecutive-years/

Valparaiso University. (n.d.-a). *Faith and learning.* Retrieved March 1, 2014, from http://www.valpo.edu/faith/

Valparaiso University. (n.d.-b). *Short-term study abroad.* Retrieved March 1, 2014, from http://www.valpo.edu/international/summer/

Wächter, B. (2003). An introduction: Internationalization at home in context. *Journal of Studies in International Education, 7*(1), 5–11.

Whitman, W. (1892). Song of myself. Retrieved from http://www.poetryfoundation.org/poem/174745

RECOGNIZING AND ADDRESSING CULTURAL DIVERSITY IN THE CLASSROOM

Today, college classrooms are made up of not only an increasingly heterogeneous body of domestic students, but also an increasingly heterogeneous body of international students, whose differing demographics, backgrounds, learning styles, and cultural mind-sets further diversify the classroom. The transnational migration of people, global media flows, and the force of new communication technologies have all become a palpable reality for international students in the U.S. university classroom today. Although global learning for many U.S. students takes place in the form of coursework with an international focus or participation in study abroad, for international students the American classroom experience itself has become a form of global learning, as they discover what it means to live, study, and engage with people from various cultural backgrounds and traditions.

In a survey of Canadian undergraduates, half of domestic undergraduates disagreed (33%) or were unsure (17%) whether the presence of international students in the classroom had enhanced their academic experience; only 14% strongly agreed with the statement (Lambert & Usher, 2013). Thirty-four percent reported that there were occasions when the presence of international students in the classroom hindered their learning (Lambert & Usher, 2013). These findings highlight the difficulty of creating inclusive classroom environments that support the learning and development of international and domestic students.

Deep learning requires sustained engagement with difference in a supportive and structured educational context. Often, encounters with difference occur by chance, but the connections among various courses and cocurricular activities could be more deliberate, connected, and pervasive across the student experience. Campuses must incorporate opportunities for students to encounter global learning at multiple points throughout college and in increasingly complex ways that progressively engage them throughout their college experience.

The student narratives presented here confirm the importance of many of the factors that are frequently cited as key to promoting cultural variation in the classroom. These include the need to adapt to a classroom culture that is more informal, professors who ask questions and expect students to respond, and professors who can act as both experts and facilitators in class (Lipson, 2008). International students appear to adapt better and achieve a quicker sense of belonging in discussion-filled classrooms characterized by a dynamic of constructive debate and disagreement, rather than in classrooms in which students listen, respectfully and silently, to a professor's lecture. Interestingly enough, the discussion and debate style of teaching often contradicts much of their previous classroom socialization.

> When you have a lecture, you just sit on your chair and you just copy everything on the board and then you have to memorize it, but now, . . . in the U.S., it isn't enough. I need to read and sometimes I say that is my opinion. I need to read even more to support my opinion, so [the U.S. classroom] gives you more opportunity and more interest to go to the library or go to different authors and try to find support for . . . your ideas. (Graduate, female from South America)

International students not only experience the shock that comes with being exposed to radically different teaching styles, but also find the informal and casual way their U.S. peers behave in classroom settings highly unexpected and even repellent.

> I think that's—It's very disrespectful to the teacher for a student to eat in class. . . . Like one time I was in class and someone was bringing a sandwich and now there's everything and people are sitting and I'm like, "Is he serious? *He's eating a sandwich in class?*" (Graduate, female from Africa)

The student's disgust in this case is particularly striking. In classrooms in many countries around the world, students are expected to rise to their feet when a professor enters the room and to address instructors by their formal title. That a person would think it appropriate to eat a sandwich during a serious lecture was abhorrent to the student we interviewed. Another student also commented on the "informality" of many American college students today:

> The first day [of class] I was like, "Is that the university or a night club?" because, you know—and I cannot even focus on what I was doing because I see, especially you know, girls dressing, their belly out, very short things. It's not that I'm against that, but it's new for me and it disturbed me a little bit. (Graduate, male from Africa)

In interviews, international students described the lived experience of participating in class and the formative role that simple classroom encounters played in their own development. The central figures in orchestrating "encounters with difference that make a difference" are professors who demonstrate a deep personal understanding of cultural variation in the classroom and create contexts that embrace that variation (O'Hara, 2009). International students tend to embrace the academic and disciplinary cultures of their American professors more readily than the informal, chaotic, and complex social cultures of their U.S. peers.

Our interviews indicated that professors provide international students with much more than academic support. Many provide essential emotional and social support, which enhances international students' sense of belonging. Positive encounters with professors, although generally transitory, contributed to the development of international students' resilience, expanded and diversified their social networks, and served as laboratories of democracy whereby international students were able to develop an independent voice, even when it contradicted mainstream class discussion. In our interviews, everyday encounters with professors—simple, taken-for-granted encounters—significantly shaped international students' sense of belonging in the classroom:

> Sometimes it's embarrassing or feeling low if you don't achieve in that subject and you're falling behind [in your] classes. In the first or second semester, I felt like, oh my God, that's too tough and you cannot do anything. . . . I approached [my professor], and he told me how to study and everything. (Undergraduate, female from Southern Asia)

It is important to note here that the professor's response emphasized the student's strength and resilience:

He encouraged me, "It's OK to have difficulties when you're studying over here and courses." He was of major help. I still meet him sometimes and say this is how it's going on, I'm about to graduate and all that stuff. He advises me on how to go on further with a job or if you want to do master's over here. . . . He has been important, crucial in my life. (Undergraduate, female from Southern Asia)

As the previous quote illustrates, classrooms are important social environments because they provide a structured domain in which to have potentially meaningful interactions with U.S. peers. At their best, classrooms today are a safe haven from, or a much-needed complement to, the informal, chaotic, and complex social cultures outside class. Relationships developed through student-to-student interactions in the structured intellectual intensity of the classroom are thus a critical feature and indispensable benefit of classroom learning.

I never thought I would be capable of doing anything like this. . . . The people I'm surrounded by kind of made me realize how people have so much potential. I have a feeling with this program I'll always need to actually develop my potential and see what I can actually do. It's just amazing. . . . Yes, I was surprised by myself, and I don't think that I would be able to do any of what I do without certain professors that basically approached me or somehow let me know that I'm good and I shouldn't be scared and I should go for it. . . . For me, the most influential person in my life from all these professors is Dr. [Professor]. (Graduate, female from Eastern Europe)

The purposeful organization of student cross-cultural interaction is another small, but significant intervention that can have profound effects on an international student's sense of belonging and inclusion in the academic environment. Another international student described the sinking feeling that she had on the first day of class, when her professor announced that students would sit at different places each class. She said,

I love talking in class and sharing my ideas with my classmates, and they'll listen to what they thought of a certain reading, for example. I think that's a big step for me. One of my professors, Dr. [Professor], what he does is he makes us sit at different places every class so we get to talk to pretty much everybody in the class over the semester. At first everybody is like, "No, I don't want to do that! That's going to suck." But then we really formed a cohesive group because of that. I love that. It makes me, again, a lot more open. (Undergraduate, female from Eastern Europe)

In this case, the professor's simple yet intentional act made it possible for the international student in question—and her classmates—to communicate with a far more diverse range of peers than she or they would have had the classroom not been structured for diversity.

The opportunity to engage in dialogue, discussion, and interaction with peers in the classroom arguably forms the core of international students' understanding of U.S. peers and even their understanding of the world at large. Dialogue, discussion, and interaction with peers are, therefore, central to what guides the development of a student's global perspective—the disposition and the capacity to take into account multiple perspectives that contribute to the formation of an authentic sense of self and help one relate to others with openness and respect (see Braskamp, Braskamp, & Engberg, 2014; Merrill, Braskamp, & Braskamp, 2012). The intensity of classroom discussions, while at times stressful, invites students to renegotiate their identity in more complex and deeply interconnected ways.

> There is not one culture but there are cultures. You cannot judge any culture based on the standards of your own culture because you'll be always wrong. Coming here then I could apply that concept. . . . Most [U.S. students] are more like . . . they try to be open-minded, try to understand that you're not coming from the same culture so they try to have an open mind about that issue and try to have an open mind about your opinion. Some of them still have this [attitude that] "what you're saying is not right; this is how it should be done and that's it; we're not trying to have a discussion here; you're wrong, I'm right" kind of stuff. Most of the time people are more open-minded about it. They try to learn about your culture [and listen] to what you're going to say than try to impose their culture on you and their point of view. (Undergraduate, male from Africa)

The connection between dialogue, identity, and self means that students, regardless of personal preference or choice, are continually faced with the need to renegotiate their social identity and perform that identity in front of others, sometimes reluctantly or unwillingly. The process of negotiating their identity, while difficult at times—even leading to tears—forges a sense of self that is more resilient and adaptable. As students reflected on their classroom experiences, they expressed a strong sense that they had become more open from these difficult encounters.

> The group would look at you [like] "What are you talking about?" I just didn't want to get that feeling so I would just let people talk, up to this year. This year I'm taking public speaking and you have to talk in front of the class, so, yeah. . . . I used to be really scared, like, when I was in front of people, I just lost all my words. I [didn't] know what to say and I just start[ed] crying. . . . [Now,] when I'm talking to them, I just smile thinking

back to when I just got here. I don't know why, but it just makes me feel, oh, I've done something. (Undergraduate, female from Africa)

International students' presence in the classroom does not in itself create a global community that enhances global learning (Leask, 2013). The stories these students shared demonstrate that there is no "neat global cosmopolitan dream" (Holliday, 2007, p. 15) and that the vernacular of the global village is much more complex as international students meet and mix with U.S. students.

> Sometimes it hurts because when you're in this country, they want you to connect or you have [to,] like, become them. That's how I would say. If you don't do that, they just left you out. They will not come to try to join you or understand. So, sometimes it hurts, but sometimes I'm just like, well I'm here to study. If I don't make people, friends on campus, I can make friends outside of campus without an attitude. (Undergraduate, female from Africa)

Language is often the first obstacle to developing supportive relationships with U.S. peers. International students tend to feel they have few shared interests with their American classmates, so American students often remain on the periphery of an international student's social network. In group work, collaborating with U.S. peers can be a reminder that friendships or relationships with American college students are typically superficial. For example, one student described her exclusion from a group-based project discussion once the topic moved to their assignment. She felt positioned as "the Other" in her group and remained silent, struggling to assert herself and unable to contribute her knowledge toward the group project.

> When there was a group project or something, you feel it—maybe there are five people in that group, you may be the only international [student], you know, there may be like four other Americans, when we are talking about the project—we are, all of us are talking, but whenever we are doing work or something, they will be interacting with each other, but they won't interact with me, I didn't do anything, I just kept quiet. (Undergraduate, female from Eastern Europe)

Unfortunately, some professors may view international students solely as students with language deficiencies, in need of extra support, or—cynically— as necessary but inconvenient revenue sources for the survival of their department's academic programs. This generates powerful dissonance between the international students' image of their university education and the behavior of some professors. Such encounters violate student expectations of being viewed as equals, and they constrict opportunities for international students to share their experiences and knowledge. Although this positioning marginalizes international students' potential contribution to classroom discussion, most students we interviewed actively resisted and disagreed with this positioning. The significant role of identity in the students' socialization and classroom experiences demonstrates the powerful link between micro, everyday interactions and larger, macro-level university cultures in which forms of structural racism persist (Bonilla-Silva, 2010):

> He thinks if you're coming from Africa, maybe you don't . . . he may think that there is no university there so if you come directly for [your] master's you may be dumb. You cannot understand anything, so it's just undermining all your abilities, all your capacities to be as efficient a student as others. (Graduate, male from Africa)

Professors, while not directly legitimizing these discourses, do indirectly and even more powerfully reinforce them through omission in silence. This student was not viewed as an equal in the classroom and described the significance of being overlooked during classroom introductions.

> For instance on the first day [the professor] was giving opportunity to his students to tell their personal experience, where they come from, what they study, what they did in life before coming to the master's program. When it comes on me, I just say my name and where I come from and then he moved to something else. I was shocked and I said I should speak even if you think my experience is not important, maybe I need to say like other students. There are many small things—but I just try to forget it but this one is kind of—the last one that I was there, it was tough for me so I decided to drop the class at the middle and my adviser tried to convince me [to leave the program] and I said no. . . . That insulted me. In other words, to [be told that] this is not your place. You don't deserve to be here. (Graduate, male from Africa)

These first-person narratives highlight international students' agency and resilience in the context of learning environments that often clash with their prior educational socialization, as well as the limited understanding and perspectives of their U.S. peers. In talking about their experiences, international students weaved multiple story lines of how they had developed and changed. Although international students are implicated in larger discourses involving intercultural relations of power and knowledge, students in their narratives identify most strongly through their stories of agency and resilience.

Overall, these narratives highlight how professors potentially provide critical emotional and social support, which enhances international students' sense of belonging. Professors' own sensitivity to cultural variation in their interpersonal encounters, in addition to inclusive classroom practices, creates a supportive classroom environment for international students. To enhance capacity for such powerful learning contexts requires deep approaches to learning among faculty members, as the next example from Valparaiso University illustrates.

Deep Learning at Valparaiso University

Valparaiso University (Valpo) prides itself on its small school environment in which direct, personal interaction with professors is integral to the student experience. The small campus provides a calm, quiet environment in northwestern Indiana, just off the shore of Lake Michigan. The school's deeper approach to student learning is also reflected in how the university prepares faculty to teach the growing number of international students on campus. Today, actively engaging international students and providing various types of support is central to maintaining the diversity that has characterized the university. For most of its 125-year history, Valpo recruited international students through personal contacts and connections. In the last several years, however, new university-to-university partnerships and purposeful recruitment efforts have resulted in exponential growth in the number of international students on campus. International enrollment has grown from 244 in 2008 to approximately 600 students in 2013. As Chuck Schaefer, chair of the International Studies Department, put it, "There has always been this global awareness emanating from Northwest Indiana. We have always had foreign students on campus, but we have seen a substantial increase in the number of international students."

One of the signature experiences at the university is the Valpo Core. The core provides a common experience to all incoming students and builds a sense of community that enlivens the academic climate for undergraduate learning. Valpo prepares all students, including international students, to actively participate in university life from their first day on campus. A warm, positive environment is cultivated well before orientation and continues through the entire first year. In each Valpo Core course, professors from various fields encourage cohorts of students to discuss major themes and ideas from human history. The Valpo Core not only stimulates student interest in study abroad; it is a key component of helping international students actively engage at the university.

Faculty members not only pay close attention to the content of the Valpo Core courses, but also pay close attention to the culture of learning these courses create. In the last several years, the institution has seen a large influx of students from China, the Middle East, and Africa. Valpo has worked to prepare faculty to engage international students in classroom learning in culturally sensitive ways. The faculty observed that often Chinese and Saudi students struggled to adapt their first year, particularly keeping up with the heavy reading load and norms of classroom discussion. These problems led the institution to adapt its Valpo Core initiative for clusters of international students. This targeted approach creates culturally sensitive, purposeful pathways into the academic environment at the university.

Schaefer has dedicated himself to discovering ways to engage faculty in the internationalization of these important first-year experiences. The department chair, whose research interests involve "indigenous methods of peace, reconciliation, and restorative justice in Ethiopia," has mapped his understanding of the politics of the diasporic Ethiopian community on to the dynamics of international student first-year experiences. Strengthening and deepening the campus's commitment to international students, in his words, "takes a huge commitment from a faculty member." Consequently, faculty development has been a core component of Valpo's unshakable focus on creating pathways for international students' academic success.

Like the international undergraduates he teaches, Schaefer was born and raised overseas and came to the United States when he turned 18. Although many universities develop initiatives that focus on helping international students adjust to learning in an American context, Valpo has approached this challenge from a different vantage point. The university encourages deep learning among faculty members in understanding today's international students. Schaefer continued, "I really need to have a deep understanding of where students are coming from." Rather than solely emphasizing the skills international students need to succeed in an American classroom, Valpo has also invested in opportunities for faculty to travel abroad to learn about the cultures of the international students they teach. Just last year, Schaefer traveled to Saudi Arabia, Iraq, the United Arab Emirates, and Oman to deepen his understanding of the cultural background of the Saudi students in his Valpo Core course. This direct, firsthand experience provided him a "deep, deep understanding of where students are coming from."

Faculty members, like all human beings, learn and grow through active engagement in direct, first-person experiences. Valpo approaches faculty development not merely as a series of units to cover in an hour-long workshop on engaging cultural variation in the classroom (as important as those are), but as through real world, face-to-face encounters in contexts of learning beyond the campus. Consequently, Valpo internationalizes the classroom not just by infusing international content but also by increasing the number of faculty exchanges abroad. Such exchanges purposefully deepen a faculty member's ability to develop culturally sensitive approaches to engaging international students from different regions of the world. Valpo's approach reflects the most current approaches to faculty development that emphasize faculty learning and professional growth. Valpo's dedication to professors' deep learning reflects a new approach to faculty work, one in which faculty members' "primary work, personally and professionally, is to learn and grow" (O'Meara, Terosky, & Neumann, 2008, p. 178). This replaces the typical paradigm of "helping students adjust to the American classroom" with a paradigm that helps faculty learn and grow new sensitivities that allow them to fine-tune their pedagogical approaches to the needs of a more globally diverse student population. Such deep learning among faculty requires an institution's ongoing commitment to enriching faculty learning and professional growth.

This approach highlights the importance of deep knowledge and understanding of the particularities of the cultural backgrounds of today's more diverse international student population. Schaefer focuses on "creating a very safe environment" for incoming Saudi students in his Valpo Core course. Many students from the Middle East, for example, are unaccustomed to offering public criticisms of government, media, or religion. Students hesitate to share what same-country peers could perceive as criticism of Saudi culture or religion. Therefore, Schaefer spends several weeks building trust so students feel free to articulate views they might otherwise hold back. By creating a safe environment, Schaefer's course allows students to listen, slowly consider the ideas presented in class, and then bring those ideas into informal discussions that occur naturally within the Saudi peer community outside class (see Leask, 2009). Students talk about the readings among themselves and feel greater comfort in exchanging ideas and opinions.

Simply throwing students into a typical debate-style classroom discussion would quickly shut down such opportunities for meaningful dialogue. The first few weeks of Schaefer's class create a safe space for such discussion to take place. The culture of the learning environment is characterized by the development of trusting relationships and an in-depth ethnic and cultural understanding of students' participating in the course. This approach necessitates a professor's finely tuned sensitivity navigating the complex social, economic, political, and interpersonal dynamics of particular students from particular cultures. Such a culturally sensitive approach matters deeply to students. Schaefer shared, "When you get to know them, and you talk to them, and you create a safe classroom environment in which they can speak, you find out that the students want to be engaged." Creating a safe space opens students to engage the tensions of their concrete lived experience: "They feel that they are sort of lucky and have to show some homage to King Abdullah, but in reality they also feel a great sense of discrimination and disenfranchisement."

Classroom Encounters With Difference That Make a Difference

College students engage in a world that necessitates productive interactions with others who hold different worldviews and come from varied cultural traditions. One thing has been made clear in the past 20 years: simply increasing the number of international students on a campus is no guarantee of internationalized curriculum. More than ever, American students have the opportunity to interact with people from varied cultural backgrounds. As the previous section illustrates, mere exposure to cultural difference in the classroom, however, is insufficient for attitude change and may even entrench U.S. students' prejudice against other cultures.

The GPI emphasizes that social context, the social and psychological environment that students inhabit, is a key driver of student development (Braskamp & Engberg, 2011; Glass, 2012; Renn & Reason, 2012). The relationships that students create through classroom interactions transcend national boundaries. Students come with diverse, complex, intersecting identities, not from monolithic cultural groups. The diversity of each student's particular social identity—including a wide variety of religious, cultural, social, ethnic, and national backgrounds—is engaged in the classroom (Hovland, 2006). Without a social context that encourages interaction, institutions will not be able to deliver on their promises of campus diversity and internationalization. International students' social relationships create a context for global learning, and classroom contexts that promote diverse interactions create new friendships and social relationships.

The GPI looks at high-impact global learning experiences, or what we call "encounters with difference that make a difference." These experiences include multicultural courses that address issues of race, ethnicity, gender, class, religion, or sexual orientation; courses that include opportunities for intensive dialogue among students with different backgrounds and beliefs; study or education abroad programs; foreign language courses; world history courses; and courses with a focus on significant global and international issues or problems (see Braskamp et al., 2014; Merrill et al., 2012).

Our research illustrates how the outcomes of encounters with difference that make a difference not only enhance students' academic performance but also enhance their sense of community, promote high-quality faculty–student interactions, and develop more complex global perspective taking (Glass, Buus, & Braskamp, 2013). Our focus on high-impact practices attempts to identify those experiences that have a particularly positive effect on students' learning and development toward civic and professional roles and responsibilities in a global society.

A decade ago, a study based on the NSSE found that international students were generally more engaged in high-impact educational experiences than were their American counterparts, especially in their first-year transition to college (Zhao, Kuh, & Carini, 2005). International students were also more likely to report a sense of academic challenge and frequent faculty–student interactions. Moreover, the study found that international students reported greater gains with respect to their learning than their American peers reported. Engagement in diversity-related activities correlated with the proportion of international students in the overall student population. Counterintuitively, however, as the number of international students increased, foreign students perceived their campus to be less supportive.

With the exception of this large-scale NSSE study, little research has been conducted on the relative degree of international student engagement in so-called high-impact practices, despite substantial research of the effects of these practices on creating inclusive campus climates for all students, and ethnic minority students in particular, as well as on improving learning and satisfaction with the college experience. Our comparisons of U.S. and international undergraduate student experiences reflect significant disparities in the quality of learning environments experienced by the two groups. Our analysis of undergraduate student data shows both signs of encouragement and other signs of concern.

For the most part, our data suggest that international students and U.S. students engage in inclusive educational practices with the same frequency. Eighty-five percent of U.S. students and 80% of international students have taken at least one course focused on multicultural issues; 40% of both U.S. and international students have engaged in a service-learning course; two-thirds of both international and U.S. students have taken a course focused on global or international issues; and 70% of international students and 65% of U.S. students have been involved in courses that involve dialogue among students with diverse backgrounds and beliefs.

Although students may enroll in courses that involve high-impact, cross-cultural learning opportunities, this does not necessarily translate into sustained interaction across ethnicities and cultures. On average, American students who took just one or two courses that involve dialogue rated their frequency of interaction with international students as rare, whereas U.S. students who have taken more than three dialogue courses are more likely to say they sometimes or often interact with students from other countries. This frequency matches international students who have taken one or even no discussion-based courses. A similar pattern exists for multicultural courses and courses that involve global or international issues.

Our research shows that the same students who rate their campus climate as inclusive and diverse participate in only a handful of multicultural courses and rarely interact with students from other countries (Glass & Glass, 2014). In other words, the most common perception among undergraduates is that their campuses are inclusive and they themselves are open to ethnic diversity despite little actual engagement in multicultural courses and few actual cross-country interactions.

Whereas U.S. students reported frequent occurrences of challenging faculty views, discussing various perspectives, and engaging faculty about their academic performance, international students did not. On average, international students reported these interactions as occurring only sometimes. International students are much less likely to believe faculty have presented issues and problems in class from different cultural perspectives or have challenged their views during class (Glass et al., 2013). Just over a quarter (28%) of international students say faculty rarely or never present different perspectives. Only one-third of international students report that faculty often or very often present different perspectives in the classroom. While almost half of U.S. students (46%) report that faculty have challenged their views during class, 30% of international students report this occurs often or very often; about half report this sometimes occurs, and 20% believe it has rarely or never occurs. Chinese and South Korean students rated the quality of these interactions lower than their U.S. peers did, and Saudi students rated the quality of these interactions as exceptionally low. Indian and Canadian undergraduates, in contrast, rated the quality of faculty–student interactions on par or even somewhat higher than their U.S. peers did.

Enhancing classroom experiences for international students requires a comprehensive approach in which global learning is deliberate, connected, and pervasive across the student experience. To create truly inclusive classroom environments, all students—both U.S. and international—must engage in meaningful global learning experiences at multiple points throughout college, as the example from FIU illustrates.

Collective Impact at Florida International University

In 2007 FIU conducted a survey that revealed that although the campus student body was diverse, the campus was not purposefully leveraging that diversity to enhance student learning in the classroom. This stimulated campus leaders to use the QEP as an opportunity to initiate a phased-in process whereby all students would take a minimum of two classes infused with global learning outcomes. These courses are designed to help students develop the ability to view the world from multiple perspectives, attain knowledge of global interconnections, and foster a desire to address local and global issues through critical thinking and problem solving. The increased enrollment of international students often necessitates that universities adapt their institutional structures to better serve international students. FIU's efforts demonstrate how an institution also can foster deep cultural change that creates a more positive campus climate.

The scale and complexity of higher education often thwarts attempts to reform the curriculum. Faculty, administrators, staff, and students are diverse sets of stakeholders that must collectively adapt their everyday routines to create a campus culture that supports global learning. Florida International University embraced its complexity by engaging faculty in internationalizing the curriculum at every stage of undergraduate education. Those leading the efforts realized that no single organization or committee, no matter who was involved, could act alone. Dr. Hilary Landorf, the director of the Office of Global Learning Initiatives and an associate professor in the College of Education, emphasized, "We endeavored to develop a network office rather than a hierarchy and to get everyone involved in creating and deciding what the learning outcomes were going to be."

Efforts to internationalize the curriculum at FIU have emphasized the key role of faculty members in leading the change. Landorf stressed, "It was our contention that in order for faculty to be able to teach the student learning outcomes, they themselves, and in fact, the university itself, had to internalize the student learning outcomes." Internationalizing the curriculum requires learning from all stakeholders, not just students. Like Valpo, FIU emphasized faculty learning and professional growth through the first-person, direct experiences of faculty members reflecting on global learning within their own fields (O'Meara et al., 2008). The university has done more than just try to get faculty on board; FIU's approach recognizes that faculty in various fields and disciplines bring their own language and emphases in curricular internationalization.

Drawing on Landorf's own interest in the connection between global learning and human capability development, the hallmark of the university's approach to global learning has been a laser-like focus on creating the conditions for *collective impact,* the "commitment of a group of important actors from different social sectors to a common agenda for solving a specific social program" (Kania & Kramer, 2011, p. 36). Social innovators have applied this approach to alleviate large-scale problems from tackling student achievement in Cincinnati; to organizing stakeholders to restore watersheds from decades of industrial pollution in southern Virginia; to preventing childhood obesity in Massachusetts; to improving health care, nutrition, and education of farmers in the Republic of Côte d'Ivoire. Drawing on models of international development from Nobel laureate economist Amartya Sen—who authored *Development as Freedom*, a capabilities approach to international development—FIU has one approach to internationalizing the curriculum that is a textbook example of collective impact (Kania & Kramer, 2011, 2013).

Higher education has a plethora of network initiatives and partnering efforts. What distinguishes efforts that focus on collective impact are five conditions for success: a "common agenda," "shared measurement," "mutually reinforcing activities," "continuous communication," and "backbone support" (Kania & Kramer, 2013, p. 1). Educational reform means "riding the waves of change" (Eckel, Green, & Hill, 1999, p. 28) in a process that creates these conditions for success. Landorf believes, "Democratic deliberation was key, and collective impact resonated with how we approach this effort."

Florida International University's approach acknowledged that internationalization encompasses many methods and interpretations depending on one's discipline, field, or professional practice. The university's process was inclusive of this diversity. For example, some faculty may emphasize *international and comparative perspectives*, involving student learning about nation-states and world regions, including the historical, political, legal, geographic, and intellectual influences on nation-states; as well as comparative studies of organizations, structures, and societies, including cross-cultural perspectives on disciplinary knowledge. Other faculty may emphasize *critical thinking about global issues*, involving student learning about quantitative reasoning, information literacy, and analytic writing skills applicable to understanding global processes that transcend national boundaries, including global media, labor markets, human rights, or environmental change. Faculty may emphasize *multicultural awareness*, involving student learning about the influence of culture, religion, gender, race, ethnicity, and other factors on identities, including issues of power, privilege, inequality, and inequity. Still other faculty members may emphasize *intercultural communication*, involving students' learning to work effectively in cross-cultural groups and multicultural settings, including opportunities for international and intercultural experiences. Finally, faculty who teach a foreign language may emphasize the importance of *proficiency in another language*, including the structure, meaning, and influence of social, cultural, historical, and political factors on language.

Collective impact "brings actors together and creates the rules of interaction that enable solutions to complex problems to emerge" (Kania & Kramer,

2011, p. 36). This approach to organizational change focuses on "creating effective rules for interaction" (Kania & Kramer, 2013, p. 4), as opposed to identifying predetermined solutions to implement. The following is how the collective impact approach played out at FIU.

The terms used to describe global learning range from *global citizenship* to *cross-cultural awareness* to *intercultural competence.* The sheer number of terms for global learning suggests that it is difficult to frame a common agenda among faculty from various disciplines. Rather than viewing this diversity as a challenge, the team leading curricular internationalization at FIU saw faculty engagement as key to enhancing global learning among its international and domestic students. From a collective impact perspective, a common agenda does not set the terms and definitions that will be in common. Instead, it frames ways for stakeholders to interact that enable the creation of a broad framework that embraces the inherent diversity of perspectives among faculty. As Stephanie Doscher, the associate director of the Office of Global Learning Initiatives, put it,

> If one of our outcomes is the ability to view the world from multiple perspectives, there's no better way to do that than to have a variety of people that see these outcomes from multiple perspectives in the same room at the same time.

Moreover, a common agenda did not spontaneously materialize. It took three years of dedicated persistent effort among stakeholders to identify a broad framework for learning that incorporated three student learning outcomes: global awareness, global perspective, and global engagement. This framework for global learning allows the Office of Global Initiatives to continuously introduce the assessment matrix as a key tool in educational assessment.

Having forged a common agenda, FIU then identified ways to measure these three dimensions of global learning in the curriculum and cocurriculum. Shared measurement does not always imply the creation of new measures. In fact, FIU used the processes and procedures already set up at the university to measure progress toward its goal. The time invested in forging a common agenda allowed the measures to flow into existing processes at the university. The university developed holistic rubrics to measure students' global perspective. Rubrics help faculty discern the learning gains of undergraduates enrolled in the two required global learning courses as compared with students not exposed to these experiences. Moreover, the Office of Global Learning Initiatives provides faculty members with reports (if they request them) that help professors learn about the effectiveness of their own approaches to infusing global learning in their courses. These reports provide faculty members with reliable data about student learning that helps them gauge the effectiveness of the interventions they design.

This flexibility is an inherent part of the third condition of collective impact: mutually reinforcing activities. Building on initial successes, an increasing number of faculty and cocurricular groups began to use the global learning outcomes, whether or not their courses carried the official global learning designation, to see how their activities reinforced this common agenda. Doscher said,

> You have to change the culture of the university. We have to provide students multiple opportunities to engage with these outcomes. . . . You cannot stop at one course. It has got to be a university-wide practice, and it has got to be curricular and cocurricular if you really want to make a difference, and you have got to involve a lot of faculty.

Florida International University recognized the deeper cultural aspects that coincide with curricular change. All directors in student affairs, for example, have also engaged the global learning outcomes and now are creating activities that develop global learning experiences that bridge in- and out-of-class learning.

Such a complex effort could not happen without continuous and open communication among the various stakeholders in these organizational change efforts. Continuous communication builds a key asset in any type of educational reform: trust. Today, hundreds of faculty members are encouraged to think about infusing global awareness, perspectives, and engagement into their coursework.

Finally, sustainable change requires a backbone organization to help diverse stakeholders work together. In the case of this change effort, the Office of Global Learning Initiatives is the backbone organization. Over several years, this office provided vision for the initiative, facilitated interaction among various stakeholders, advanced global learning as a priority, and secured funding from the university that ensured the initiative would continue. Without this backbone organization, faculty members would have never been brought together. There would have never been a shared approach to measurement. Simply put, collective impact is impossible without the support of a backbone organization. Doscher concluded,

> The Office of Global Learning Initiatives in our university is the backbone organization that is apart from the stakeholder participants, but facilitates communication, assessment, sustains the initiative over the long term, brings stakeholders together to design and to implement different aspects of the initiative. We're just that, we're the backbone organization for our initiative.

Conclusion

This chapter highlighted the role that classroom encounters play in the social and academic integration of international students. The campus examples from Valpo and FIU show how enhancing interactions among international and domestic students requires supporting faculty professional growth and making global learning more deliberate, connected, and pervasive across the student experience—for all students. Courses that invite international students to engage in dialogue, discussion, and interaction with peers enhance their sense of community, promote high-quality faculty–student interactions, and develop more complex perspectives. Although international and U.S. students engage in inclusive educational practices with the same frequency, international students are much less likely to believe faculty have presented issues and problems in class from different cultural perspectives or have challenged their views during class. While most of the international students we interviewed recounted student–faculty interactions that created a sense of inclusion, negative experiences left lasting impressions. In the next chapter, we discuss cocurricular experiences that contribute to cross-cultural interaction and an enhanced sense of belonging among international students and highlight the important role of leadership programs in this process.

References

Bonilla-Silva, E. (2010). The style of color blindness: How to talk nasty about minorities without sounding racist. In *Racism without racists: Color-blind racism and the persistence of racial inequality in the United States* (pp. 53–74). New York, NY: Rowman & Littlefield.

Braskamp, L. A., Braskamp, D. C., & Engberg, M. E. (2014). *Global Perspective Inventory: Its purpose, construction, potential uses, and psychometric characteristics.* Chicago, IL: Global Perspective Institute. Retrieved from https://gpi.central.edu/supportDocs/manual.pdf

Braskamp, L. A., & Engberg, M. E. (2011). How colleges can influence the development of a global perspective. *Liberal Education, 97*(3/4), 34–39.

Eckel, P. D., Green, M., & Hill, B. (1999). *Riding the waves of change: Insights from transforming institutions.* Washington, DC: American Council on Education.

Glass, C. R. (2012). Educational experiences associated with international students' learning, development, and positive perceptions of campus climate. *Journal of Studies in International Education, 16*(3), 226–249. doi:10.1177/1028315311426783

Glass, C. R., Buus, S., & Braskamp, L. A. (2013). *Uneven experiences: What's missing and what matters for today's international students.* Chicago, IL: Global Perspective Institute.

Glass, C. R., & Glass, K. R. (2014). *Going against the herd: Social ecologies of multicultural engagement in college.* Philadelphia, PA: American Educational Research Association.

Holliday, A. (2007). *The persistence of constructions of superiority and inferiority in cultural description.* Unpublished manuscript, Canterbury, UK.

Hovland, K. (2006). *Shared futures: Global learning and liberal education.* Washington, DC: Association of American Colleges and Universities.

Kania, J., & Kramer, M. (2011). Collective impact. *Stanford Social Innovation Review, 9*(1), 36–41.

Kania, J., & Kramer, M. (2013). Embracing emergence: How collective impact addresses complexity. *Stanford Social Innovation Review, 11*(4), 1–8.

Lambert, J., & Usher, A. (2013). *The pros and cons of internationalization: How domestic students experience the globalizing campus.* Toronto, ON: Higher Education Strategy Associates.

Leask, B. (2009). Using formal and informal curricula to improve interactions between home and international students. *Journal of Studies in International Education, 13*(2), 205–221. doi:10.1177/1028315308329786

Leask, B. (2013). Internationalizing the curriculum in the disciplines: Imagining new possibilities. *Journal of Studies in International Education, 17*(2), 103–118. doi:10.1177/1028315312475090

Lipson, C. (2008). *Succeeding as an international student in the United States and Canada.* Chicago, IL: University of Chicago Press.

Merrill, K. C., Braskamp, D. C., & Braskamp, L. A. (2012). Assessing individuals' global perspective. *Journal of College Student Development, 53*(2), 356–360. doi:10.1353/csd.2012.0034

O'Hara, S. (2009). Vital and overlooked: The role of the faculty in internationalizing U.S. campuses. In *Meeting America's global education challenge* (pp. 38–45). Washington, DC: Institute for International Education.

O'Meara, K. A., Terosky, A. L., & Neumann, A. (2008). *Faculty careers and work lives: A professional growth perspective* (ASHE Higher Education Report, Vol. 34). doi:10.1002/aehe.3403

Renn, K. A., & Reason, R. D. (2012). *College students in the United States: Characteristics, experiences, and outcomes.* San Francisco, CA: John Wiley & Sons.

Zhao, C.-M., Kuh, G. D., & Carini, R. M. (2005). A comparison of international student and American student engagement in effective educational practices. *Journal of Higher Education, 76*(2), 209–231. doi:10.1353/jhe.2005.0018

2

ENGAGING INTERNATIONAL STUDENTS IN CAMPUS LEADERSHIP

Many universities highlight opportunities for international students to make American friends, engage in international activities, and participate in leadership programs. Although university activities that engage students across cultures are plentiful, cross-cultural experiences are the products of serendipity, and many international events are poorly attended because of limited interest from domestic students. Even if some international students connect across cultures in meaningful ways, many still feel disconnected.

Renowned Harvard political scientist Robert Putnam examined the issue of trust within communities of ethnic diversity. Putnam (2007) found that more ethnic diversity in a local community is associated with less trust both within and between groups. His findings indicate that less trust is associated with fewer close friends, less confidence in one's ability to influence others, and less motivation to work on community-oriented projects. The mere presence, then, of more international students and underrepresented student groups on campus is in no way a guarantee that the benefits of diversity will be produced. Contact without a context—fleeting, unstructured—may instead be more likely to exacerbate prejudice, lower confidence in one's ability to influence the views of others, and undermine any expectation that diverse student individuals and groups can cooperate to solve mutual problems (Hanassab, 2006; Pettigrew, Tropp, Wagner, & Christ, 2011; Schmitt, Spears, & Branscombe, 2003).

Leadership programs at U.S. universities and colleges teach students to anticipate with curiosity how encounters with diverse identities will strengthen their capacity to solve problems. Purposeful, targeted, and well-timed interventions help international students make sense of their experiences, send strong signals of inclusion, and have a ripple effect on students' academic trajectories. These effects are also amplified over time. When students feel more secure, they engage more actively in the classroom environment, build cross-cultural relationships, express greater confidence in constructing knowledge with others, and create a stronger platform for their academic success in college.

Often, leadership programs have a practical focus on problem solving, event organization, leadership development, or areas of professional interest. These programs offer encounters with difference that do not tackle difference directly. Instead, they allow international students to "sidle up to difference" (Appiah, 2011, para. 3). Rather than facing differences head-on, students first learn to talk about an issue of mutual professional interest or work together to plan a campus event. Both U.S. and international students may not talk about cultural and ethnic differences directly or frequently. Yet, they get to know one another. Rather than engaging in an abstract and potentially conflictual discussion about Islam, a U.S. student might instead befriend a Muslim student organizing a campus event. These connections help to replace a vague sense of a monolithic "them" with the concrete reality of another person's life story.

International Students' Engagement in Leadership Programs and Community Service

The GPI data demonstrate the importance of leadership programs in fostering cross-cultural engagement among students. Leadership programs create social contexts that bridge students' social networks and forge the connections between otherwise distantly connected people. They represent what sociologists call "small world networks"—places where strangers are linked by shared acquaintances (Watts, 2004). This phenomenon suggests something profound: that each of us is connected to people with whom we have absolutely nothing in common (Christakis & Fowler, 2011). Often, the benefits of close relationships are highlighted in research that deals with international student adjustment (e.g., Lee, Koeske, & Sales, 2004). However, weak ties through small world networks can also have an important effect (Hendrickson, Rosen & Aune, 2011). Although our social networks tend to cluster along the divides of socioeconomic class, religion, and nationality (McPherson, Smith-Lovin, & Cook, 2001), leadership programs allow those who are normally divided from each other to exist a relationship or two away from one another.

Increased engagement in cocurricular activities greatly affects international students' sense of belonging and in turn enhances their desire for and degree of cross-cultural engagement. For the most part, the GPI data suggest different patterns of involvement among international students and U.S. students when it comes to cocurricular activities (Glass, Buus, & Braskamp, 2013). In general, participation in leadership programs is the most commonly reported cocurricular activity among all students, domestic and international. About one-third of U.S. and international students participates often or very often in leadership programs, about one-third participates occasionally, and one-third participates never or rarely. Interestingly enough, our analysis of the 2009–2013 GPI data showed that Indian students had the highest participation levels in leadership programs, surpassing even the participation levels of U.S. students. Forty-five percent of Indian students surveyed reported participating often or very often in leadership programs, whereas 38% of U.S. students agreed that they participate often or very often. Saudi students, in turn, are the least likely to participate in leadership programs, with a mere 13% reporting frequent participation in such programs.

Community service ranks second among the most frequent forms of cocurricular engagement among U.S. and international students, with one-third of U.S. students and 30% of international students reporting that they participate often or very often in such activities. According to our analysis of GPI data, students from India participated in more community service projects than their U.S. peers, with over half (54%) reporting that they took part in community service often or very often. Not surprisingly, international students reported participating in lectures, workshops, and campus discussions on international issues more often than their U.S. peers, 25% and 15%, respectively. About half of international and U.S. students reported that they never or rarely attend a campus lecture, discussion, or workshop. U.S. students reported participating in spiritual or religious activities slightly more often than international students, 23% and 17%, respectively. Over half of international and U.S. students never or rarely participate in spiritual or religious activities.

Leadership programs are not only the most popular type of cocurricular activity among U.S. and international students alike; they have also been shown to have a significant impact on other aspects of campus life (Glass et al., 2013). What happens outside the classroom, including participation in leadership programs, appears to affect what happens in the classroom. Our analysis of the GPI data showed international students who reported that they rarely engaged in leadership programs also reported that they rarely engaged with faculty members and rated their overall sense of community as more neutral (Glass et al., 2013). International students who occasionally participated in leadership programs engaged with faculty members more frequently but still reported a neutral sense of community. However, international students who participated in leadership programs often or very often reported engaging faculty members often and felt a stronger sense of community.

International Students' Experiences in Leadership Programs

Many of the international students we interviewed specifically stated that they came to the United States to face challenges that they anticipated would help forge an independent self—to develop a sense of perseverance and confidence that only emerges after a long and difficult journey. The movement away from friends, family, cultural traditions, language, and social networks reflects international students' self-understanding within the framework of resilience and agency, despite the inevitable frustration, loneliness, isolation, and marginalization that they may encounter and need to overcome.

In this context, leadership programs become important encounters with difference that are important because they enable international students to find common ground with and develop connections to peers whom they might otherwise overlook or never meet. Moreover, leadership programs expose international students to difference in the form of other students' first-person stories. These different forms of encounters with other students in a structured setting enhance not only international students' understanding of other cultures, but also their interest in and willingness to engage in cross-cultural encounters:

> It allowed me to communicate with people that are totally different, really different, that in my everyday life, I would never talk to them or never approach them. They would just seem weird or strange, but I got the chance to meet them and to get to know them. I regret that I used to judge people by the way they look or they dress, but now I don't anymore. I think you need to talk to someone to communicate with them, instead of just judging them by their appearances. . . . It's like you learn how to accept the others no matter how different they are, no matter what their sexual orientation is, their thoughts, religion, belief. It's just so diverse, you just learn how

to accept people. First, we listen to others, their stories, their experiences. When you hear it from them, you realize that these people have become stronger and have become what they are now because of these experiences and these stories. (Undergraduate, female from Africa)

As this student narrative suggests, the transformative effects of leadership programs come, at least in part, when international students are able to encounter other students' first-person accounts for themselves. In the following passage, one of the students interviewed describes the profound effect that these indirect encounters had on his view of the world around him:

On the personal basis, I gained a lot, the way I think about other people, other religious beliefs, other backgrounds, so that positively changed my view of the different people because when you meet people only then you'll realize their way of thinking, their beliefs. If you just study the books or listen to the media, you get their interpretation, you don't get the real people because you are learning them from a third source. When you meet them in person and you talk to them, only then you come to know their real value and their real face. It changed my way of thinking about people from other backgrounds, other religious backgrounds, other cultures. I feel that it will help me making rational decisions my whole life. . . . Yes, it totally changed my perspective of looking into the world differently, but you are talking about when the people think that I changed, so yes. They already think that I changed in so many ways, yes. (Graduate, male from Southern Asia)

There are no quick fixes for the damaging academic and social consequences of negative stereotypes and reflexive anxieties about a particular social group or category (Spencer-Rodgers & McGovern, 2002; Steele & Aronson, 1995). Nonetheless, leadership programs that facilitate intercultural interaction in settings characterized by the four basic elements of Allport's (1954) contact hypothesis—equal status of the groups in the situation, common goals, intergroup cooperation, and the support of authorities—do appear to reduce intergroup anxieties and prejudice (Pettigrew et al., 2011). The support of authorities—in this case, culturally sensitive student affairs staff—has been shown to create a context in which students can safely explore the nature and impact of identity differences:

Maybe that's one of the most beautiful experiences in the U.S., because I feel so lucky to be with people from different countries, talking in a very friendly way, and people who [are] also interested about your culture. Not because they want to fight or argue, just because they want to know your way to live or way to think about the situation. [The university] has this environment that allows you to have conversations about different opinions and beliefs without putting you in a difficult situation. I feel safe with my culture, and I think that other people feel as [I do]. You can be Muslim, you can be Buddhist or Catholic, you don't have any problem. If you believe in socialism or capitalism or liberalism, you don't have any problem with that. (Graduate, female from South America)

Leadership programs also provide international students the individual and collective capacity to advocate for their interests, as the campus example from ODU illustrates.

International Student Advisory Board at Old Dominion University

Recently, an article on health insurance options for international students at U.S. universities and colleges appeared in *Inside Higher Ed* (Redden, 2013). In the comments section, one international student posted the following:

We are the ones who pay for the coverage and schools often force us to buy the school plan by coming up with ridiculous requirements. For example, the school I'm attending now . . . requires that I have coverage for inter-scholastic, intercollegiate sports in order for them to accept my PSI Plan. I did not come to the U.S. to become a college athlete. I'm here to get my PhD. Now, is it fair for me to pay $3,000 for the school plan where I can get a comprehensive plan for $1,500? Most of us international students are aware of these kinds of tactics that schools do to get us to buy the school plan and the majority of us don't complain because we got our student visa status with the help of the school. This is sad but a reality. (Zhang, 2013)

Comments like this suggest that international students are more aware as consumers of a U.S. education than many stakeholders in U.S. higher education realize. It also indicates that many international students are beginning to find it necessary to speak out on issues that concern not only the quality but also the cost of their U.S. educational experience.

Too often, however, the campus power dynamics that shape the international student experience get ignored (Gargano, 2009). The lack of attention by many U.S. universities to the challenge that rising health insurance costs pose for international students is one major concern, but by no means the only concern, that today's international students have. International students often have issues unique to their situation, such as a lack of adequate campus food options, a lack of student employment opportunities, intercultural conflicts with roommates, and problems finding adequate housing. When administrators listen to these concerns with a deaf ear or dismiss international students as a niche student subpopulation, some international students have organized themselves to ensure their voices are heard by their university. The ISAB at ODU is an example of political organizing that promises a new model of university–international student relations:

> The International Student Advisory Board (ISAB) represents the ODU international student community and provides constructive feedback to the Office of Intercultural Relations (OIR), Office of International Programs (OIP) and other university departments. The ISAB not only offers suggestions for improving current programs and services, but also makes recommendations for new initiatives. (Wongtrirat, 2012, p. 1)

Originally launched as a small initiative within ODU's Office of Intercultural Relations (OIR), the ISAB has substantially increased its influence on campus. During its first year, the board provided feedback to the OIR on international student programming and suggested ideas for additional programs and services. However, as it began to receive negative comments from ODU's international student community on various issues, such as on-campus employment opportunities, housing, and the skyrocketing cost of health insurance, the ISAB adopted a more focused, action-oriented stance and mission. Under the guidance of a faculty adviser, the ISAB transformed from a small forum along the lines of a university suggestion box to an advocacy group engaged with senior university administrators about issues of significant concern to international students. As part of this mission, the ISAB makes recommendations regarding current and proposed university policies and suggests initiatives aimed at enriching the campus life of ODU's international student population.

The ISAB's faculty adviser, appointed jointly by the executive directors of the OIR and Office of International Programs (OIP), works with 20 board members to proactively address issues of concern to international students. To broaden its focus beyond intercultural programming, the ISAB developed a formal mission, a board, terms of service, and an application process. The board organized subcommittees around five persistent issues of concern: housing and public safety; student life and cultural integration; financial and administrative concerns; public relations; and academic performance. The ISAB focuses on developing board members' knowledge, capacities for negotiation, networking, relationship building, and leadership as it builds coalitions around salient issues. Since the ISAB is not a student organization, it is free to act without adhering to certain policies and procedures that might constrain its ability to function independently and decisively.

In addition to its work with ODU administrators, the ISAB also hosts an open forum during which international students can air and share their grievances about the university's response to concerns particular to the international student community. In 2012 the ISAB took on the issue of rising health insurance costs, arguing that the policy unnecessarily required international students to purchase platinum health care. Offering a greater range of cost and health care coverage options would be more equitable and reasonable. The ISAB subsequently organized a united international student group requesting sufficient explanation of this policy and the rapidly rising costs of health insurance for international students. This action eventually encouraged the university to reexamine the policy and to allow an ISAB member to serve on its health insurance committee. In short, political pressure from the ISAB prompted administrators to respond more actively to international student concerns than they might have otherwise.

The creation of the ISAB at ODU also demonstrates the importance of social capital in campus political organizing. A well-run board requires the support of a strong faculty adviser. A strong adviser understands how to navigate the political dynamics of both the university and the international student community and has developed sufficient status and relationships at the university to be effective. Today, the ISAB's existence crystallizes and legitimizes the concerns of international students. It organizes otherwise disparate voices into one coherent and collective voice that speaks to other campus stakeholders and, in turn, directly to the administration. This organizational capacity has allowed international students at ODU to experience a greater sense of agency than before, which has also resulted in a greater sense of belonging and willingness to raise other issues that might otherwise have gone uncommunicated. Although dissent caused short-term disruption for ODU administrators, in the longer term, international students have expressed greater satisfaction and trust in the institution, thus strengthening the relationship between ODU and its international student community. International students at ODU now feel more engaged and personally responsible for creating a positive campus climate for themselves. They are more empowered to contribute to comprehensive internationalization at ODU because they have a welcoming forum for pointing out gaps and tensions as well as for discussing issues that previously went unaddressed. Moreover, international student board members have forged stronger relational bonds with each other and developed valuable leadership skills through their ISAB experience.

Whereas the ISAB initiative at ODU illustrates the importance of building international students' individual and collective capacity to advocate for their interests on campus, the community service initiatives at Valencia College illustrate how this capacity extends beyond campus. Among other initiatives, Valencia uses purposeful intergroup encounters to increase students' intercultural knowledge, empathy, and capacity for taking a global perspective.

Connecting Campus and Community at Valencia College

Valencia College is a multicultural campus; students are used to being surrounded by people from diverse backgrounds and cultures. Just over half (54%) of students are native English-speaking, and almost one-quarter are native Spanish-speaking. This compositional diversity allows Valencia to weave a rich educational environment that engages students with opportunities to learn more about other cultures and "to learn about the world without having to travel the world" (B. Thompson, personal communication, July 18, 2013). In a recent institutional study, an astonishing 97% of students sampled expressed comfort interacting with peers from others cultures. Students date across cultures (Robertson, in press), and they have cross-cultural roommates. Yet, like all the campuses we highlight in this book, Valencia was not satisfied, even with such strong results. The college continues to look for ways to improve and enhance intercultural interactions among students. To do so, international educators surveyed students to explore the academic and personal backgrounds that contributed to their capacity for global perspective taking. They discovered that three things contributed to global perspective taking among students: direct encouragement from professors; participation in international activities, including taking courses from professors who incorporate global topics into the course content; and interaction between international and domestic students that is facilitated by professors.

Valencia reflects the public purposes of higher education as structures align, cultures transform, and the institution organizes itself to demonstrate an active commitment to its local community. As Benson, Harkavy, and Puckett (2007) advocate in *Dewey's Dream*,

> Higher education institutions must give full-hearted, full-minded devotion to the painfully difficult task of transforming themselves into socially responsible civic universities and colleges. To do so, they will have to radically change their institutional cultures and structures, democratically realign and integrate themselves, and develop a comprehensive, realistic strategy. (p. 84)

The transformative effects of community engagement through active research, teaching, and service partnerships continue to have great potential in revitalizing the public purposes of higher education in society.

Although Valencia has a long history of international education, its efforts, like those of many institutions, seemed disconnected—the result of higher education's disjointed, siloed institutional structures. For years, continuing education, student affairs, and academic affairs each separately advanced internationalization efforts at the college. However, a major challenge was that the efforts were fragmented across different areas. The early impetus for change came in 2011, when stakeholders across the college developed an international education strategic plan linked to the college's values and goals. The combined efforts of this team led to a greater visibility of the college's work in international education. Momentum picked up significantly when, in the fall of 2012, the president spurred the institution to look for new ways to work collaboratively across different initiatives. This led to the reorganization of the international student services area.

Today, the restructuring has put international student services under the auspices of Continuing Education in order to capitalize on a highly structured and well-managed international student recruitment system. International students no longer get bounced around from office to office. Each campus now has an international student services office where students know they can go to whenever they need anything. The office is a safety net in difficult times, a place to get social support, and a connection point for resources that help international students remain resilient throughout their education at Valencia. International students are assigned a counselor who acts as a first line of defense in bolstering their resilience by providing practical, psychological, and social support. International advisers give academic and immigration advising, assist students with enrollment, and provide personalized attention to students' psychosocial adjustment. Valencia, through its reorganization and strategic focus on international education, is "on the brink of changing the culture," and today, international students are now a vital part of "enhancing the environment for the college" (J. Robertson, personal communication, July 18, 2013).

Taking the college's characteristically cooperative approach, the international office built a relationship with the internship office so students could participate in practical experiences related to their majors that connect them with the surrounding community. Not only do these internships tie international students to community members, they also internationalize the local community through student engagement. Just as Elon University (highlighted in the next chapter) organizes groups of international and domestic students to engage across cultures through study away experiences, Valencia assembles groups of international and domestic students in powerful community partnerships. As Rocky Blesso, director of International Student Services at Valencia, said, "International students, and I think all of us actually, tend to flock to secure groups. So one of our goals is to get students intermixed with the domestic population and with each other." Valencia leverages its community partnerships to enhance public understanding and provide community service opportunities for its diverse student population.

For Valencia, this focus on engagement involved looking for new ways to enhance intercultural interaction. In the next academic year, International Student Services' goal is to create programs that will allow international students to foster public understanding of global cultures by speaking in the local community as well as on campus to student organizations and classes. An initiative titled Valencia International Peers (VIPs) will be one such program. Currently, the Intensive English Program at Valencia promotes intercultural understanding by providing cultural excursions as part of its cocurricular activities. Such excursions are also in the plans for degree-seeking international students. The international educators at Valencia recognize that "it is intimidating for an international student to jump out there and participate individually in the community, but when they can participate as a member of a group they are more confident and successful" (R. Blesso, personal communication, July 18, 2013).

Often, campus leaders focus on how to connect international and domestic students. Valencia is a model example of how those connections begin with campus leaders themselves, combined with strong coordination across offices. The strong relationships and new structures, combined with a significant investment of resources and staff, helped the campus organize and align its activities to create a more integrative, experiential, and meaningful learning environment for its diverse student population. The college has become a place that is itself diverse, with multiple campuses spread across Central Florida. It has connected this diversity in a way that lets international students connect with U.S. students and the local community. The leaders are taking an active approach. They communicate with partners, present issues about the international student population, and engage academic advisers, staff members, and senior leaders. This approach allows everyone to understand the issues international students face. These offices then work together to forge partnerships that enhance, strengthen, and deepen the international student experience. The campus leaders we interviewed described this approach as "taking the bull by the horns, so to speak; get out there and start talking about this population, and start creating some of the synergy we're looking for."

As a result of new structures, a new strategy, and new investments, the campus has been able to create a climate in which international and domestic students are encouraged to fully engage in international education initiatives, particularly through the internationalization of the curriculum as a way to "make a broader impact to the overall education and preparation of our students in the twenty-first century" (J. Robertson, personal communication, July 18, 2013). These international experiences, whether local or abroad, change lives, create opportunities, and play an essential role in higher education in the United States. Valencia has made it a priority to create opportunities for international and domestic students to interact, learn, and work together, through the connections between the college and the local community.

In summary, institutional leaders created change by acting on two key observations: international education has a central role to play in enhancing education for all students, and the Valencia campus had not realized its full internationalization potential. The institution subsequently placed the academic and social integration of international students at the top of its agenda and transformed a visibly fragmented, siloed system into a cohesive and integrated partnership between diverse offices. By focusing on the public purposes of international education, Valencia has seen substantial institutional change in the span of a few short years. The leaders connected the purpose and traditions of the institution with its ongoing process of comprehensive internationalization. This enabled Valencia to promote a culture of inclusiveness, community engagement, and respect for the diverse experiences that its student body contributed to the process of building the academic community.

Conclusion

This chapter highlighted how leadership programs greatly enhance international students' sense of belonging and, in turn, strengthen their desire for and degree of cross-cultural engagement. Leadership programs help international students find common ground and develop connections with peers whom they might otherwise overlook or never meet. International students who participate in leadership programs more actively engage in the classroom environment, build cross-cultural friendships, and forge cross-campus ties that support their academic success in college. We illustrated the ripple effects of these programs with examples from ODU and Valencia. Leadership programs not only enhance international students' individual and collective capacity to advocate for their interests on campus; community-service leadership programs also increase students' intercultural knowledge, empathy, and capacity for global perspective taking. In the next chapter, we describe the role of friendship in international students' well-being and academic success.

References

Allport, G. (1954). *The nature of prejudice.* Cambridge, MA: Addison-Wesley.

Appiah, K. A. (2011, August 4). Sidling up to difference: Social change and moral revolutions. *On Being.* Retrieved from http://www.onbeing.org/program/sidling-difference/transcript/558

Benson, L., Harkavy, I., & Puckett, J. L. (2007). *Dewey's dream: Universities and democracies in an age of education reform, civil society, public schools, and democratic citizenship.* Philadelphia, PA: Temple University Press.

Christakis, N. A., & Fowler, J. H. (2011). *Connected: The surprising power of our social networks and how they shape our lives.* New York, NY: Back Bay Books.

Gargano, T. (2009). (Re)conceptualizing international student mobility: The potential of transnational social fields. *Journal of Studies in International Education, 13*(3), 331–346. doi:10.1177/1028315308322060

Glass, C. R., Buus, S., & Braskamp, L. A. (2013). *Uneven experiences: What's missing and what matters for today's international students.* Chicago, IL: Global Perspective Institute.

Hanassab, S. (2006). Diversity, international students, and perceived discrimination: Implications for educators and counselors. *Journal of Studies in International Education, 10*(2), 157–172. doi:10.1177/1028315305283051

Hendrickson, B., Rosen, D., & Aune, R. K. (2011). An analysis of friendship networks, social connectedness, homesickness, and satisfaction levels of international students. *International Journal of Intercultural Relations, 35*(3), 281–295. doi:10.1016/j.ijintrel.2010.08.001

Lee, J.-S., Koeske, G. F., & Sales, E. (2004). Social support buffering of acculturative stress: A study of mental health symptoms among Korean international students. *International Journal of Intercultural Relations, 28*(5), 399–414. doi:10.1016/j.ijintrel.2004.08.005

McPherson, M., Smith-Lovin, L., & Cook, J. (2001). Birds of a feather: Homophily in social networks. *Annual Review of Sociology, 27*, 415–444. Retrieved from http://www.jstor.org/stable/2678628

Pettigrew, T. F., Tropp, L. R., Wagner, U., & Christ, O. (2011). Recent advances in intergroup contact theory. *International Journal of Intercultural Relations, 35*(3), 271–280. doi:10.1016/j.ijintrel.2011.03.001

Putnam, R. D. (2007). E Pluribus Unum: Diversity and community in the twenty-first century. The 2006 Johan Skytte Prize Lecture. *Scandinavian Political Studies, 30*(2), 137–174. doi:10.1111/j.1467-9477.2007.00176.x

Redden, E. (2013, September 17). Buyer beware. *Inside Higher Ed.* Retrieved from http://www.insidehighered.com/news/2013/09/17/colleges-fear-international-students-are-purchasing-inadequate-health-plans-private

Robertson, J. (in press). Student interest and participation in international education at the community college. *Community College Journal of Research and Practice.*

Schmitt, M. T., Spears, R., & Branscombe, N. R. (2003). Constructing a minority group identity out of shared rejection: The case of international students. *European Journal of Social Psychology, 33*(1), 1–12. doi:10.1002/ejsp.131

Spencer-Rodgers, J., & McGovern, T. (2002). Attitudes toward the culturally different: The role of intercultural communication barriers, affective responses, consensual stereotypes, and perceived threat. *International Journal of Intercultural Relations, 26*(6), 609–631.

Steele, C., & Aronson, J. (1995). Stereotype threat and the intellectual test performance of African Americans. *Journal of Personality and Social Psychology, 69*(5), 797–811.

Watts, D. J. (2004). *Six degrees: The science of a connected age.* New York, NY: W. W. Norton.

Wongtrirat, R. (2012). *The International Student Advisory Board (ISAB) mission statement and policy* [PDF document]. Retrieved http://www.odu.edu/content/dam/odu/offices/intercultural-relations/docs/ISAB_description.pdf

Zhang, Li. (2013, September 17). Re: Buyer beware [Web log comment]. Retrieved from https://www.insidehighered.com/news/2013/09/17/colleges-fear-international-students-are-purchasing-inadequate-health-plans-private#comment-1048000618

3

FRIENDS, PEERS, AND
SOCIAL NETWORKS

When asked where he came from, Diogenes, the ancient Greek philosopher, famously replied, "I am a citizen of the world." This first known use of the word *cosmopolitan*, which derives from the Greek word *kosmopolitês* (citizen of the world), departed from the Greek notion of one's identity as attached to a particular city-state, or *polis*. Fundamental to the concept of cosmopolitanism today is the notion of an identity that is not attached to a particular nation-state but rather belongs to and functions in plural, diverse worlds (Calhoun, 2003).

Traveling to the United States provides an opportunity for international students to participate in transnational networks—social networks in which day-to-day interactions involve people from two or more countries (Gargano, 2009). People who engage in such diverse and geographically disperse networks often have more in common with each other than with peers living in their home country or with U.S. students (Bhatia & Ram, 2009; Fong, 2011). The friendship networks forged by these students invite us to consider the depth as well as breadth of the transformation occurring as students across the world become increasingly globally mobile. In what follows, we argue that their sense of belonging to liminal transnational social networks that span institutions, localities, and nation-states complicates any traditional understanding of what being "an international student" is like or means today. Indeed, the student narratives included in this chapter reveal a multiplicity of trans-spatial identities and relationships that have fundamentally reshaped international students' lives today and changed the ways that they interpret their U.S. student experience.

Mapping International Students' Social Connections

Almost 90% of international students in the United States report that they have felt very lonely at their respective universities and have turned to international social networks for social support (Smith & Khawaja, 2011). Understanding the way that international students are connected to others is essential if universities are going to be able to implement relevant, user-friendly policies and programs that improve the health, well-being, and quality of intercultural interaction among all of their students. A network perspective draws our attention away from the individual as the unit of analysis to consider how the overall structure of a network affects an international student's experience.

The social networks of today's international students are characterized by an intricate web of relationships consisting of strong kinship ties, friendships at their home institution and abroad, and distant acquaintances that make up an important periphery of their network (Blau & Fingerman, 2010). The journey abroad for international students often necessitates leaving strong family and kinship ties at home and exchanging them for weaker connections with U.S. peers abroad (Montgomery, 2010). Thanks to the Internet and the more recent explosion of wireless technologies, some of the most intimate ties that international students have remain with their friends and family members living abroad, whereas some of their most distant relationships may be with peers sitting next to them in class (Anderson, 2013). In spite of the rise of the network society, once international students go abroad to study, physical as well as social distance separates them from full and immediate access to the social capital networks of home, which means that they cannot as easily connect with family, friends, and others for the social support they once enjoyed. As such, international students' friendships with same-institution peers still serve as a critical means of personal advancement, both socially and academically (Poyrazli, Kavanaugh, Baker, & Al-Timimi, 2004).

The international students we interviewed described at great length the support that they received from friendships with fellow nationals as well as other international students. The university experience created an opportunity to engage in a uniquely cosmopolitan environment, much like a small city, that provided a social context in which students' educational and social aspirations were often fulfilled in very different or unexpected ways (Koehne,

2006). For some international students, the university experience allowed them to feel like a tourist on an extended trip; for others, the university was a forum in which to generate future business partnerships; and for another group, attending a U.S. university generated a generalized sense of connectedness to a globalized world. Finally, some international students explained that their university experience allowed them to explore other cultures, which helped them to become more self-reflective about the limitations of a culturally homogeneous or mono-ethnic identity.

> The best thing is this country or education here is it's not only American. You can meet all the people in one place, so you get all the culture while you are in one place. (Graduate, male from the Middle East)

> When I get out of my hotel, I look at people and I see that they are diverse, because in my country you cannot have all people but here you have Asians, Latinos, Americans, Africans, African Americans. You have the world like in a small scale. (Graduate, male from Africa)

Our interviews also revealed that international students often play an active role in forming supportive learning communities that help their members to achieve academic success. Such communities also serve as a forum for international students to share the history of their journey as well as their emotions and experiences, from orientation to graduation. A strong sense of a shared in-group identity thus emerged among an otherwise differentiated group of international students. This combination of practical and social support has been shown to be a key factor in international students' adjustment, acculturation, and academic success (Smith & Khawaja, 2011).

Friendships among a diverse network of conational and international student peers also gave these students access to practical information that the participants we interviewed used on a regular basis to make their lives easier and better while studying in the United States. Among other things, students received help from each other about navigating the complexities of university bureaucracy, finding public transportation, and finding groceries and clothing. Our interviews with international students confirmed that U.S. universities often serve as unique, if sometimes unintentional, cosmopolitan spaces in which international students who are otherwise worlds apart find themselves at home together: "What strikes me the most is I didn't really feel alien in the U.S. I didn't feel like I was not home. I was just not home, but not foreign. It was in-between" (Graduate, male from Eastern Europe).

As international students navigate these new and complex social environments, most of those we interviewed acknowledged a sense of being in-between. Like other kinds of migrants, these students felt they were at a temporary station, wedged between different life spaces (e.g., home and away) and characterized by immense diversity and hybridity. Amid this flux, the international students we interviewed described meaningful friendships as ones marked by consistency, trust, and helpfulness stemming from a sense of common values, interests, and experiences. As these students discovered, friendship styles, and the meaning of friendship itself, can vary significantly according to a student's ethnic and cultural background (Gareis, 1995). Close friends were defined as those who took an interest in the daily experiences of the international student. In contrast, acquaintances—most often Americans—were defined as those who showed less interest in these experiences. This has also been a regular finding in the literature on international students' relationships with their U.S. peers (Gareis, Merkin, & Goldman, 2011). According to the same international student quoted previously,

> I felt actually pretty good and I made friends with both American and international friends. Friends, if you define friends as acquaintances, also someone I know versus someone that I got really friends with in the States. I did have really good friends, a couple of them who are Americans and who are international. There are a lot of acquaintances and there are more American acquaintances than international. (Graduate, male from Eastern Europe)

While international students in our study frequently characterized U.S. peers as kind or helpful, U.S. students rarely played a role in their stories about significant relationships or events. The deep and essential relationships formed among conational and international students stand in stark contrast to the activity-filled, short-term, and shallow relationships that most of the international students interviewed indicated having with American peers. In our interviews, international students described friendships with U.S. students as less engaged, more ephemeral, erratic, and unpredictable:

> I wouldn't say I have a whole lot of American friends, actually. I don't know, I don't need them. (Graduate, male from Southern Asia)

> Speaker 1: Why don't you tell me about your international and American friends?
> Speaker 2: I guess I'm going to start with my American friends because I don't have much. (Undergraduate, male from Africa)

> I don't have many American friends. My best friends are international. Well, I've connected with some of my classmates, but it's not a very deep relationship. It's like a friend I can stop by and say, "Hi, how are you?"—have a

little conversation. It's not a deep friendship. (Undergraduate, female from Eastern Europe)

I have international friends. I know American people, but we're not close friends. I have a lot of international friends. (Undergraduate, female from Africa)

Here I have, I tend to—I don't know why—but it's international friends—I mean real friends are always foreign. (Undergraduate, female from Western Europe)

I think most close friends, for me, most close is international, not American. (Undergraduate, female from Africa)

For international students, you can't really go and hang out with American people—I don't know, we want to be friends, but there is something that— we don't—we are not really friends. (Graduate, male from Asia)

I don't know why it fails. I cannot really . . . I cannot come up with a big reason . . . why most of relation between international and Americans fail, but I feel like usually it fails. (Graduate, male from Africa)

Indeed, the list of complaints about relationships with U.S. peers is long: Americans are parochial, they party and drink, they are rude to their parents, they show little interest in other cultures, they do not demonstrate respect to professors, and they are not serious students (see Williams & Johnson, 2011). Moreover, many of the international students we interviewed spoke specifically about examples of American friendliness, such as inviting an international student to one's dorm room for coffee, that international students mistook as a sign of interest in developing a closer friendship. When this proved not to be the case, many students we interviewed spoke of dashed expectations, hurt, and the feeling of having been duped or even betrayed by their American peers. For most of the international students we spoke with, friendships with American peers lacked the steadfastness, sustainability, and also predictability that would allow for the natural growth of a true friendship over time. Rejection by American peers, although hurtful and unpleasant, was often juxtaposed by international students in our interviews with the unexpected and welcome proliferation of more substantive friendships with other internationals:

I thought, "I'll go there, I'll study, and then I'll get my degree; then that would come towards something." Then when coming here, then going to the events, and then you meet people from different cultures, not just international like American people, do you know about their culture too; what they think about us too; what they know about our country too. That kind of changes your perspective in a way, because I hear people, you hear things, and you kind of have this notion that people might be like this and people might be like that. You have that in your mind. You cannot say, "I'm not. I don't judge people." You cannot be like that, because you see things, you hear about it, so it's like okay. Then when I came and that's—right now, when I look back, I think I have grown in that. I thought I was a pretty open-minded person, but after coming here and meeting . . . people, I became more open-minded in that sense, like trying to understand other people from where they come from rather than just assuming my own ideas. When I just came in, I didn't expect that to happen. I thought I'll just come in, go to classes, get my degree and be done with it and people like—maybe I'll talk with people from [my home country], and I'll just be done with it. The expectation was nothing at all, like, nothing in terms of growth, except academic. (Graduate, female from Southern Asia)

I have bunch of friends from all part of the world. I have friends from Japan, Korea; I have friends from Australia; I have friends from Pakistan, Afghanistan, Bangladesh, Sri Lanka, Uzbekistan, Russia, Ukraine; I have friends from Poland, Slovakia. (Graduate, male from Southern Asia)

At times, this proliferation of international relationships among international students results in the sense of being a stranger—of not belonging the way that native U.S. students appear to belong. At other times, the international students we interviewed talked of the ways in which inclusion in these transnational social networks of friends and future colleagues expanded their sense of possibility as well as connection to their respective universities. In other words, attachment to a university had little or no basis in traditional, place-bound notions of campus spirit, pride, and university traditions for these students. Instead, this sense of attachment was forged through their participation in the transnational student networks that emerged out of their university environments. These are networks that U.S. universities are uniquely positioned to enable as well as to foster, if they so choose.

The diversity of the university. You find all people from everywhere, and I think that's a really good thing. You don't feel like you're a stranger, even though you don't belong here, but you feel that you're a part of the university, which is a good thing. That's what I like about [the university]. (Undergraduate, female from Africa)

When international students in our study described the elements of a close relationship, they frequently stressed the importance of being able to confide in one another, of offering voluntary and practical support for someone in need, and of sharing similar experiences as a form of demonstrating emotional support.

> My international friends, they're amazing, actually. They know what I have been through because we all had the same experience. They understand me sometimes. I never thought that I would have this many international friends when I was back in Morocco. I never thought that I'd know people from Spain, England, Scotland, Asia. It's a great opportunity, it's a great experience. (Undergraduate, female from Africa)

Making friends across cultures is no doubt complex, varying from individual to individual as each person is confronted with unfamiliar social norms. For most international students, the formation of intercultural friendships reflects both the durability of their national identity and the expansion of their understanding of how that identity connects with other identities across the globe (Foong, 1999; Marginson, 2013). In fact, the formation of friendships with other international students has a paradoxical effect—deepening a student's own ethnic and national identity, while at the same time opening him or her up for a globalized identity that is not exclusively connected to a specific nation-state (Bhatia & Ram, 2009; Phelps, 2013): "Yeah, and I have been friends with almost all of the international students, and I know about their cultures, and we share everything, so I feel I'm an international student right now, not just an Indian student" (Graduate, male from Southern Asia).

Belonging Nowhere and Everywhere

For international students, the new friends, peers, and social networks that accompany crossing borders open up new possibilities. The international student narratives presented in this book repeatedly give expression to the identity struggle that most, if not all, international students are likely to face. They are neither fully at home nor fully rooted in their host collegiate community. As such, they must constantly negotiate who they are and who they are not as they navigate life both inside and outside the classroom.

The personal narratives in this chapter provide concrete examples of how international students navigate this "in-between" identity as they encounter cultural boundaries that range from generalized feelings of difference to disruptive experiences that evoke a sense of being out of place, of being an outsider and other, of being foreign. Lai Heng Foong, an international student from Malaysia, illustrates this complexity. In her personal memoir included in the essay collection *Crossing Customs: International Students Write on U.S. College Life and Culture,* Foong (1999) describes her sojourn from Malaysia to Canada and later to the United States. She writes, "I believe that one's identity can be formed and reformed and that who I am is constantly in flux" (p. 208). Her memoir provides a powerful depiction of the complex personal and social challenges encountered by international students as they cross cultural boundaries, negotiate them, and develop greater resilience and self-reliance as a result.

> I said that I belong nowhere but I think it is more accurate to say I try hard to feel I belong everywhere. I tend to seek out what I find appealing in different cultures that I am exposed to and gradually incorporate those qualities into my own personality. I believe that one's identity can be formed and reformed and that who I am is constantly in flux. In a dynamic process of change, I no longer feel exclusively bound by culture, nationality, or background. Reliance on myself has made it easier for me to adapt to new surroundings because I am not constantly trying to define my place in relation to where I was before. Instead, I try to reconcile myself to a new home by relying upon myself which provides a constancy that is needed in an unfamiliar environment. Finding solace in the familiarity of oneself provides a welcome sense of permanence. . . . In myself, I feel at home. (p. 208)

A growing number of scholars have further argued that as the spatial reality of international students changes, so too does the spatial reality of the universities they attend (Gargano, 2009). If international students come to U.S. universities and colleges enmeshed in fully operating transnational social networks of kith and kin, the universities that serve them may need to find new ways to interact with and engage these students, both academically and on campus. Indeed, universities must begin to understand and respond to the fact that they are now one actor among many that inhabit the transnational social fields of today's international students, not the other way around (Bhatia & Ram, 2009; Gargano, 2009). U.S. colleges and universities may therefore need to focus more resources on learning how to identify, navigate, and support these complex environments in order to better serve their international students. Recognizing the influence of these transnational networks will enable international educators and administrators to more successfully harness their power in order to promote the academic success and personal growth of the international students they serve.

The International House at Northern Arizona University

Not only individuals but even groups of international students may feel distant or isolated from other student groups and sense that that they lack access to the larger cultural life of the university. The international house (I-House) at Northern Arizona University (NAU) is one example of how purposeful initiatives on a university's part can bring previously unconnected student social networks together in one place, establish a new conduit for conveying much-needed student resources and practical information, and provide a new and welcoming forum for students to forge new international relationships.

The idea of an "international house," a place where students from around the world live, study, and eat together, was born on the steps of the Columbia University library. A young YMCA employee, Harry Edmonds passed a Chinese student sitting on the steps of the library. Edmonds offered a conventional greeting, "Good morning." The Chinese student, stunned at being spoken to, responded, "I've been in New York three weeks, and you are the first person who has spoken to me" (International House, n.d., para. 1). Edmonds approached John D. Rockefeller Jr. and the Cleveland H. Dodge family with an ambitious vision to create residential gathering places for foreign graduate students. By the early 1930s, international houses in New York City, at the University of California–Berkeley, and in Chicago attracted foreign students from around the world.

The first international house opened in New York City in 1928. It quickly became a hub for social and community gatherings for graduate students from around the world. The University of California–Berkeley pioneered a model of the potential for international and intercultural living. At a time when people of color and "whites" drank at different water fountains, the International House at the University of California–Berkeley was a radical proposal. John D. Rockefeller, who helped fund the house, created it so students had "the full opportunity for frank discussion on terms of equality, the importance of which it is difficult to overvalue" (Bevis & Lucas, 2007, p. 87). International houses continue to be hubs of cultural exchange that are central to campus internationalization initiatives.

The I-House at NAU, staffed by a hall director and nine residence assistants, opened in fall 2012. It is part of NAU's larger vision for comprehensive internationalization. Like international houses across the United States, the aim of the I-House residence is to help domestic and foreign students gain awareness of global issues, practice speaking foreign languages with native speakers, and foster curiosity and appreciation of different cultures. This intercultural living environment prepares students to live and work abroad, to engage as community leaders, and to communicate cross-culturally. It has quickly attracted students from around the globe interested in sharing in Culture Nights and participating in community service events in nearby Flagstaff, Arizona. Like their predecessors in New York, Berkeley, and Chicago, students in the I-House are matched by interest in learning about a particular culture or language.

Although international houses are nothing new, NAU has taken a purposeful approach by integrating its international house with its Global Science and Engineering Program (GSEP). The GSEP, a five-year dual-degree program, integrates language and culture into the typical engineering and science curriculum. Program students spend an internship year abroad in China, Japan, Latin America, or Europe at one of NAU's partner institutions. The I-House provides a critical opportunity for GSEP students to consolidate their language skills and practice living and working in a multicultural environment. These students have the opportunity to practice what they have learned in the classroom in a supportive living–learning environment.

One of the unique aspects of the I-House is its goal to place international students with American students who are fluent or studying their native language. Ninety percent of the American students in the I-House are fluent in a second language or studying a second language at NAU. Americans students are, therefore, able to get an international, cross-cultural experience before they study abroad. Likewise, international students in the I-House know they will be placed with an American roommate who has a genuine interest in learning to live and work in a cross-cultural environment. These two aspects of living in the I-House give comfort to international students because they know they will be living with an American student who has an interest in their culture and language. In comparison, international students who do not live at the I-House tend to be placed with students from their home country or transfer students, who may not share the same level of interest in living cross-culturally.

Betty Leask (2009) suggested that international educators "move away from deficit models of engagement, which position international students as interculturally deficient and home students as interculturally efficient, when both need support" (p. 218). The I-House does just that. Domestic and international students engage one another in daily conversations and interactions that develop each other's intercultural competency. The four-person suite-style hall allows the flexibility to put an American student who is studying German with a German student in one room and an American student who is studying Chinese with a Chinese student in the other. This permits some diversity within the suite as well.

Dylan Rust, the program director of the I-House, makes a point to build cross-institutional partnerships and connect residents of the I-House with other entities at NAU. According to Rust, "Partnerships are a really big deal, and students learning from students is important." Currently, the institution is looking for opportunities to bring the I-House to scale, where it can serve larger populations of domestic and international students. Attracting well-qualified American students, about 40% of the I-House population, has been central to the success of the I-House initiative. Partnering has been central to the I-House's success. Rust emphasized,

> I first try to amplify what's already being done on campus and work with that, as opposed to trying to do everything yourself. It's more beneficial for the students to partner with other international and cultural events and entities at the institution. Not everything has to be from the ground up.

The strong partnership with the GSEP has been one of the most important connections Rust has developed. Rust described partnering, including collaborations with colleagues in housing and residence life, targeted engagement of domestic students in language or culture courses represented in the I-House, and partnering with international student admissions, as the key to the I-House's success. NAU is currently developing an initiative to track alumni of the I-House and follow the long-term impacts of this purposefully constructed living–learning environment. Additionally, current students can engage the worldwide I-House alumni network to find potential work opportunities.

Harvey Charles, vice provost for international education at NAU, emphasized the financial and administrative resources required for an initiative like I-House to work. NAU does not treat international students as a "cash cow"; it reinvests additional tuition revenue into strengthening the quality of its international programs. At a recent Association of American Colleges and Universities conference on global learning, Charles argued,

> It is a mistake to believe that funding comprehensive internationalization is a cost that cannot be afforded. The exact opposite is true. A well-resourced internationalization infrastructure means that there are resources to fund global learning projects and other university priorities. In fact, making an investment in comprehensive internationalization can actually generate even more resources. (Cited in Redden, 2013)

The I-House is an example of devoting infrastructure and resources to ensure purposeful cross-cultural learning takes place; across-campus partnerships have been central to the success of NAU's comprehensive internationalization strategy.

An Uneven Sense of Community

A recent GPI survey (Glass, Buus, & Braskamp, 2013) focused on the uneven experiences of U.S. and international students at U.S. universities revealed that although U.S. students believe their campuses honor diversity and internationalism, they themselves rarely or never interact with students of other nationalities. This finding notwithstanding, U.S. and international students responded similarly to items about their general attitudes to people from other ethnic and cultural backgrounds. The vast majority of U.S. and international students indicated that they enjoy learning about cultural differences, feel confident in their ability to take on various roles in different cultures, and express openness to people with lifestyles different from their own.

The difference in patterns of social interaction among U.S. and international students is evident in their actual behavior and friendships. Seventy percent of international students who responded to the GPI reported interacting with cross-country peers often or very often, while only 40% of U.S. students report interacting with cross-country peers often or very often. These findings corroborated from the report "The Pros and Cons of Internationalization: How Domestic Students Experience the Globalizing Campus":

> Over 90 percent of students thought that international students were welcomed on campus; however, only 72 percent said they thought that international students themselves felt included in the campus, which suggests that, from a student perspective, being welcomed and being included are not quite the same thing. (Lambert & Usher, 2013, p. 7)

Moreover, 40% of international students who responded to the GPI reported that most of their friends are from ethnic backgrounds different from their own; another 40% reported that most of their friends share their ethnic background, and 20% reported a mixture of friendships somewhere in between. Conversely, only 20% of Americans reported that most of their friends come from different ethnic backgrounds than their own, 60% reported that most of their friends share the same ethnic background, and 20% reported a mixture of friendships somewhere in between.

Given these findings, it may come as no surprise that on every measure of sense of community, international students rated their campuses lower than their U.S. peers did. International students reported less of a sense of affiliation with their university; they were less likely to agree that their campus honored diversity and internationalism; they felt less challenged and supported by their university, and they were less likely to believe they had been encouraged to develop their strengths and talents at their college or university (Glass et al., 2013). Most strikingly, survey results indicated that international students felt that they lacked a close and supportive community. While U.S. students generally agreed that they were part of a close and supportive community, international student responses were far more neutral. This lack of community on campus was especially pronounced among students from China, Saudi Arabia, and South Korea (Glass et al., 2013).

The capacity to engage with peers across countries and to see the world from unfamiliar perspectives requires opportunity, focus, practice, and sustained dialogue. Purposefully structured cocurricular activities, such as leadership programs, offer a clear context for intergroup encounters and thus become a particularly important catalyst for attitudinal change. The Study USA initiative at Elon University represents one such example of a purposeful, institutionally driven activity contributing to the creation of encounters with difference that make a difference.

Study USA at Elon University

The United States is one of the most diverse countries in the world. At Elon University, almost three-quarters of students study abroad, a signature experience woven into the curriculum as part of the university's epic comeback. Like those at all the institutions we highlight in this book, the senior leaders at Elon looked for key leverage points that infused the entire curriculum in order to strengthen and deepen its commitment to international students. The faculty and administrators identified ways to ensure that engaging in a global experience was central to all students' education. Phil Smith, director of Study USA at Elon, demonstrated the university's commitment to ensuring that all students have a global education experience when he stated,

> In 2013, 72 percent of our graduating class had a study abroad experience which means 28 percent did not. We asked ourselves, "What can we do to get those 28 percent to have some sort of intentional encounter with difference, something we have termed a global experience?" You can have the same type of experience—a disorienting encounter with cultural practices and stories unlike yours.

International students often arrive with a desire to engage and communicate with the local people and community. Opportunities to engage in the city and culture, as well as travel opportunities, are among the most prominent factors that motivate international students to study in the United States. One of the key influencers of student satisfaction is the general atmosphere of the city of the university. International students desire opportunities to make connections with nearby cultures and opportunities to explore local norms and ways of thinking.

From a desire for continuous improvement, Elon designed a Study USA program that combines the best of the practices that the GPI identifies as having a significant impact on students' global perspective: experiential learning, study abroad experiences, opportunities for intensive dialogue among students with different backgrounds and beliefs, and multicultural encounters. The Study USA program puts international students and domestic students on a road trip together for a semester to study a local culture. Rather than international students being "the outsiders," all of the students in the experience travel and stay together. Collectively, they are the outsiders to the community that they study and engage. According to Phil Smith,

> I would hold the Study USA experience against some of our international programs as students are in the thick of things in a community for up to 21 days in our winter term programs, and up to a full semester in some programs. The essays students write about their cultural learning, which I am always excited to read, rival some of our study abroad essays.

Deep engagement incorporates multiple experiences with peers sustained for a time, and some of the most transformative experiences are within the vicinity of the university itself. Many international students come from large cities, so the opportunity to engage in small, rural American towns for an extended period is a tremendous experience for encounters with difference that make a difference. For example, in one Study USA experience, students travel to rural Kentucky to engage a small coal-mining town. International and domestic students spend 21 days encountering the local culture, sharing the experience of being outsiders, and encountering cultural practices and human stories unlike their own. Study away experiences also include travel to large cities like Los Angeles, New York, and Washington, D.C., but focus on a localized area of the city. When students travel to New York, for example, they spend nine weeks completing an ethnographic study of a street or a small part of the city. Students see the lives of the people they encounter from a different vantage point than tourists. They take photos, interview people, discover the history of individual buildings, capture people's stories, and learn the dynamics that shape the local economy. International students also learn the history of race relations in America in a program called Discovering Dixie. A political science professor takes students on a bus, stopping by the roadside to point out places that have meaning in America's racial history and explaining everything from the Revolutionary War and Civil War to modern-day social, economic, and political dynamics that affect race relations in America.

Study away experiences give domestic and international students an up-close history of the United States not accessible in a traditional classroom. Whether students travel to a small coal-mining town, conduct an ethnography on the streets of New York, or explore Southern history and culture on a roadside tour, the travel of a diverse group of students facilitated by a professor creates an "eyes wide open, tremendous experience" (P. Smith, personal communication, July 23, 2013) that integrates classroom and real-world learning opportunities.

The design of these experiences is the key to Elon's success. Any faculty member may propose a Study USA course by outlining goals in three main areas: academic content, cultural awareness, and personal growth. Elon draws on its rich heritage in crafting transformative study abroad experiences to extend those opportunities to the 28% of students who do not enroll in a traditional study abroad course, including a large proportion of international students. The group dynamics created by Study USA encounters facilitate intercultural learning among the students in the program as well as between students and their local environment. Professors identify study away locations and outline culture-related content, involving history, politics, geography, art, or economics. They then identify ways to facilitate students' understanding of the significance of the culture in which they are immersed and develop a deepened awareness of cultural variation within the United States. Finally, professors identify ways to spark students' intellectual curiosity, encourage self-awareness, and foster personal growth.

Students deeply engage the local norms, people, and customs directly. The design of the Study USA experience allows students from diverse backgrounds to discover commonalities and become open to hearing their peers' diverse points of view. This encounter with difference makes a difference because it is equally foreign to all group members. Learning is enriched by students hearing their peers' diverse reactions to the collective experience. The power of these experiences derives from the potent combination of encounters with difference that make a difference over a sustained period: dialogue and discussion and multicultural encounters. Such experiences forge intercultural friendships among students with diverse backgrounds and experiences.

Conclusion

This chapter has had several aims. First, it attempted to highlight the qualitative aspects of students' relationships to one another that contribute to their sense of personal as well as campus belongingness. Second, it aimed to examine the role, or lack of role, that American students play in the international student experience at U.S. universities today and the similar absence of international students in the lives of American college students. A third aim has been to highlight some of the ways in which U.S. universities have become new sites of cosmopolitanism in an age of rapidly increasing global student mobility and network technologies growth. The cosmopolitan connectedness of today's international students is proving a challenge to universities everywhere and on several fronts. It challenges universities to reassess their relationship to a rapidly expanding and incredibly diverse student demographic. It challenges universities to reassess, if not actively reconstruct, the nature of the relationship that exists on campus and in class between domestic students and their international students peers. Finally, it challenges universities to implement relevant, user-friendly policies and programs that can improve the quality of intercultural interaction among all students and, thereby, their sense of well-being and belongingness on campus and in the classroom. In the following chapter, we discuss in more depth how the use of social media with home- and host-country peers affects international students' sense of belonging in particular.

References

Anderson, K. (2013). *Anthropology, globalization, and higher education* (Unpublished master's thesis). University of Wisconsin–Madison, Madison, WI.

Bevis, T., & Lucas, C. (2007). *International students in American colleges and universities: A history*. New York, NY: Palgrave Macmillan.

Bhatia, S., & Ram, A. (2009). Theorizing identity in transnational and diaspora cultures: A critical approach to acculturation. *International Journal of Intercultural Relations, 33*(2), 140–149. doi:10.1016/j.ijintrel.2008.12.009

Blau, M., & Fingerman, K. L. (2010). *Consequential strangers: Turning everyday encounters into life-changing moments*. New York, NY: W. W. Norton.

Calhoun, C. (2003). "Belonging" in the cosmopolitan imaginary. *Ethnicities, 3*(4), 531–553. doi:10.1177/1468796803003004005

Fong, V. L. (2011). The floating life: Dilemmas of education, work, and marriage abroad. In *Paradise redefined: Transnational Chinese students and the quest for flexible citizenship in the developed world*. Stanford, CA: Stanford University Press.

Foong, L. H. (1999). Finding solace in the familiarity of myself. In J. Davis & A. Garrod (Eds.), *Crossing customs: International students write on U.S. college life and culture* (p. 191–209). New York, NY: Routledge.

Gareis, E. (1995). *Intercultural friendship*. New York, NY: University Press of America.

Gareis, E., Merkin, R., & Goldman, J. (2011). Intercultural friendship: Linking communication variables and friendship success. *Journal of Intercultural Communication Research, 40*(2), 153–171.

Gargano, T. (2009). (Re)conceptualizing international student mobility: The potential of transnational social fields. *Journal of Studies in International Education, 13*(3), 331–346. doi:10.1177/1028315308322060

Glass, C. R., Buus, S., & Braskamp, L. A. (2013). *Uneven experiences: What's missing and what matters for today's international students.* Chicago, IL: Global Perspective Institute.

International House, University of California–Berkeley. (n.d.). *History.* Retrieved March 1, 2014, from http://ihouse.berkeley.edu/about/history.php

Koehne, N. (2006). (Be)Coming, (Be)Longing: Ways in which international students talk about themselves. *Discourse: Studies in the Cultural Politics of Education, 27*(2), 241–257. doi:10.1080/01596300600676219

Lambert, J., & Usher, A. (2013). *The pros and cons of internationalization: How domestic students experience the globalizing campus.* Toronto, ON: Higher Education Strategy Associates.

Leask, B. (2009). Using formal and informal curricula to improve interactions between home and international students. *Journal of Studies in International Education, 13*(2), 205–221. doi:10.1177/1028315308329786

Marginson, S. (2013). Student self-formation in international education. *Journal of Studies in International Education, 18*(1), 6–22. doi:10.1177/1028315313513036

Montgomery, C. (2010). *Understanding the international student experience.* New York, NY: Palgrave Macmillan.

Phelps, J. M. (2013). *"I'm just in-between somewhere": Transnational graduate students in the globalized university.* St. Louis, MO: Association of the Study of Higher Education.

Poyrazli, S., Kavanaugh, P. R., Baker, A., & Al-Timimi, N. (2004). Social support and demographic correlates of acculturative stress in international students. *Journal of College Counseling, 7*(1), 73–82.

Redden, E. (2013, October 7). Grappling with global learning. *Inside Higher Ed.* Retrieved from http://www.insidehighered.com/news/2013/10/07/conference-focuses-integrating-global-learning-within-curriculum

Smith, R. A., & Khawaja, N. G. (2011). A review of the acculturation experiences of international students. *International Journal of Intercultural Relations, 35*(6), 699–713. doi:10.1016/j.ijintrel.2011.08.004

Williams, C. T., & Johnson, L. R. (2011). Why can't we be friends? Multicultural attitudes and friendships with international students. *International Journal of Intercultural Relations, 35*(1), 41–48. doi:10.1016/j.ijintrel.2010.11.001

4

FAMILY RELATIONSHIPS, TECHNOLOGY, AND SOCIAL MEDIA

Important networks of family relationships, largely hidden from view, are a central feature of an international student's capacity to remain resilient, since these relationships temper many of the risks and challenges that the student confronts while studying abroad. Host universities must therefore be prepared to approach international students both as individuals and as representatives of their extended family networks. Indeed, it is often these unrecognized networks that provide key emotional support for the student and even bear the cost of his or her college education, thus making the possibility of international study realizable (Hamberger, Houseman, & White, 2011).

Family and Kinship Networks' Views of Self and Identity

In addition to the narratives of the students themselves, the narratives of entire family, partner, and sibling networks were a major component of the experiences of the international students we interviewed. Indeed, these students' experiences were frequently embedded within the larger migration narratives of their entire family and kinship networks. Anthropologists Suarez-Orozco, Darbes, Dias, and Sutin (2011) emphasize the importance of kinship relations in the daily lives of international students:

> Distinct patterns of kinship, household, family, and social organization are of paramount importance in structuring worldwide migratory waves. The fundamental unit of migration is the family variously defined in different parts of the world and structured by distinct culturally coded legislative, economic, reproductive, and symbolic forms. At the manifest level, immigration may be driven by labor, demographic, economic, and environmental variables. However, below the surface, immigration's enduring root is the family. Immigration is an ethical act of, and for, the family. Immigration typically starts with the family and family bonds sustain it. Immigration will profoundly change families as well as the societies in which immigrants settle. (p. 313)

For many international students, the act of studying abroad is the product of a collective effort of diverse extended kinship networks coming together to further that student's education (Pimpa, 2005). These complex kinship networks help international students navigate the immigration process, investigate potential universities to attend, educate students about what to wear, and share the risks that may be associated with migration.

At the same time, an education in the United States, particularly for middle-class families, is expected to result in tangible benefits for the family as a whole—not just the student. Although the parents of international students often absorb most of the financial cost of their child's college education up front, this cost may also be distributed among multiple family members. This kind of extended familial financing of a college education binds students not only to their parents, but also to their extended family. Equally important, such a cost-sharing arrangement binds the student's host university to that family, as illustrated by the account of an international student from India in Anderson's (2013) analysis of the distribution of risks, costs, and benefits of international study across kinship networks:

> There aren't maybe too many expectations, but if I earn that much then I'll definitely pay them back. I just want to—they should be in a comfortable position. So if I'm earning then we'll always help them out. And I think that's how things in India work. The parents support their kids and then kids support back to parents. It's like give and take. (p. 55)

Without a network of extended family members, international study simply would not be possible for many international students. Fong (2011), for example, highlights examples of students from poor and working-class families that distribute the risks as well as the potential financial and social rewards of sending a young family member abroad. Consequently, universities are implicated in relationships, not just with individual, fee-paying international students, but also with entire extended family networks. Networks of extended family members bear the economic risks of investing in a family member's international study. International students and their families do not necessarily perceive an education abroad solely as the private good that it represents to many U.S. students and their families. More than just the individual benefits of a higher-paying job for the international student, families anticipate the potential social, political, and economic benefits from strengthened transnational connections (Anderson, 2013).

Traditionally, attending a U.S. university has meant in loco parentis, supervision by the institution in place of a parent (Chickering & Kytle, 1999). At the same time, parents, extended family members, and globally dispersed kinship networks are instrumental in allowing international students to move and act within the university environment while also remaining connected to each other (Birnbaum & Gonzalez, 2012; Yan & Berliner, 2011; Ye, 2006). These networks foster a sense of belonging that transcends university boundaries. For many international students, then, social integration is not merely a matter of "fitting into college" in the traditional, place-bound sense of the phrase. Instead, their social life is oriented more toward a dispersed network of family relations that has no physical bearing on the host campus:

> When I talk about my family, I tend to think about my direct family and [my husband's] family. But, the truth is that I have a lot of very often contact with *my* family, with both of my parents, with all of my sisters. When I say very often, like, at least once a week. And it's more than that because we Skype a lot and we Google Hangout, whatever works better, depending on the mood of the Internet. . . . We say, good morning, have a nice day. That's every single day with my dad and with my sisters. We have different groups. We have this group with my dad and my sisters. We have a group just with my sisters. . . . I talk with [my grandparents] too, especially with her. My grandpa will say "Hi!" and then disappear. And then with my in-laws. . . . Very often, it's an important support. To be able to talk with them and to say whatever. I had a good day or today this happened, to be able to communicate it. (Anderson, 2013, p. 61)

Finally, it should be noted that not all international students who study in the United States migrate in order to pursue their own education. Many international students experience a "double adjustment" (De Verthelyi, 1995, p. 403)—both cultural adjustment and an adjustment to new social roles within a family structure—as one spouse leaves a career to support his or her partner's decision to study in the United States. Some spouses may pursue an advanced degree at a U.S. university because of limited work and financial options resulting from visas that prohibit them from seeking employment. Other spouses may be relegated to domestic responsibilities. For example, in Anderson's (2013) study of the experiences of international families, one of those interviewed was Somi (pseudonym), who had a PhD in physics from her home country. Despite an advanced degree, she had severely limited opportunities for advancement within her chosen field in the host country:

> With the F-2 visa there is nothing that I can do. I cannot even go to the English school. And I cannot work. So that makes me a little bit frustrated and a little bit, how can I say, bored? And I kind of became a little bit . . . what is that . . . to feel, um, lonely. . . . So I was just, maybe I can take like a four year break because he came here one year earlier than me. Maybe I have like four years and then I can be a good homemaker, and I have some organic food and I can learn how to cook, how to manage the home. And I thought that I will really enjoy that life. But actually, I can't. (p. 40)

Like Somi, international spouses, both female and male, may find themselves negotiating marginalizing roles within their families when they relocate to another country to enable their partner to study or work there. Such roles may render them, as in Somi's case, a "wife who just sits at home" (p. 66) and is "made [to feel] invisible" (Teshome & Osei-Kofi, 2011, p. 65). Legal constraints and restrictions in the host country are thus often additional factors that contribute to feelings of loneliness, isolation, frustration, and depression among the partners of international students (Teshome & Osei-Kofi, 2011). Despite the challenges of double adjustment, research on international graduate students also indicates that students with a partner experience less strain in the process of social and cultural adjustment than their single graduate student counterparts (Poyrazli & Kavanaugh, 2006).

Networked Families

Today, international students and their families lead very connected lives. With the growth of inexpensive wireless media and communication technologies, the increased use of social media in general, and the relatively low cost and greater accessibility of global travel, international students are now able to maintain much closer and more sentient relationships with family and friends back home (Elliot & Urry, 2010; Ye, 2006). Despite great distances, then, family members in multiple localities around the world can remain intimately connected with one another if they so choose. International students are thus able to seek support from a complex, if virtual, network of cousins, siblings, and friends living both abroad and throughout the United

States (Murphy, 2008). Thus, international students today no longer simply exist "here" at the university and have their families "there" in their home country. Instead, these students experience a "simultaneity of locality and multiplicity in identities" made possible by the rise of global mass travel and the technologies they use (Gargano, 2009, p. 337).

Today, many international students and their families go online together to re-create family togetherness. The ability to share multimedia clips and moments of "Did you see that?" creates a form of shared experience that allows all parties to maintain a fundamental sense of continuity and connectedness. Here are two typical examples of student responses to one of our open-ended interview questions, "When you need support, where do you find it?"

> My parents, no hesitation. My parents and my oldest sister. That's it. (Undergraduate, female from Africa)

> My family. Skype is my number one friend. [Laughs.] (Undergraduate, male from Southern Asia)

No international students we spoke with referred to this ongoing communication with family members as intrusive or disruptive to their college experience. The safety of knowing that a family member—a cousin, a brother, a sister, an uncle, a mother, or a father—was only seconds away in a moment of crisis allowed the international students we interviewed to take risks and to share, or distribute, the consequences of these risks among their kinship networks.

Family members far away were in turn able to assume significant roles as monitors, mentors, and supporters of these international students (Rainie & Wellman, 2012). The ability to Skype with a cousin, to call a grandfather, or to ask advice from an uncle living across the country in the United States enabled international students to avoid feeling isolated from others. It also allowed them to maintain access to important human sources of advice and information that helped them to manage practical daily issues.

From this perspective, retreating to one's dorm room to use the Internet to access a local newspaper or to post a comment on a friend's Facebook wall is not necessarily an asocial activity, but rather an important ritual that maintains cultural and personal connections. In fact, the contention that international students' use of social media further isolates them from national students was not at all evident in our conversations. On the contrary, secure relationships with supportive family members far away enabled international students to explore cross-cultural relationships with their peers on-site. Indeed, many international students cited the importance of social networking sites such as Weibo, Facebook, or LinkedIn in helping them to connect with U.S. peers and other international students, many of whom they planned to maintain contact with after graduation (Lin, Peng, Kim, Kim, & LaRose, 2011).

Technology was not only a critical means of connection between the international students we interviewed and members of their extended family a state or a continent away. As the next initiative from IU illustrates, technology is also a tool that empowers universities to monitor, adapt, and respond proactively to issues that affect the academic success of international students.

Getting the Basics Right at Indiana University–Bloomington

John Wooden, the legendary University of California, Los Angeles (UCLA), basketball coach, emphasized the basics and even spent time helping new players learn how to tie their shoes. The basics, after all, are often the essential but boring keys to success. It is important to have solid practices and policies in place. Getting the basics right has been essential to serving international students at Indiana University–Bloomington (IU). IU experienced phenomenal growth in the number of Chinese students attending the institution; its Chinese population skyrocketed from 1,000 in 2009 to almost 3,000 in 2012—three times the students, three years later. The university has also seen a major shift in the proportion of undergraduate international students, which grew from a little over one-third of its total international student population to well over one-half (56%) of international student enrollment. IU has a long history in international student exchange, is one of the top-10 destinations overall for international students who study in the United States, and has the fourth-largest undergraduate international student population in the country.

Christopher Viers, associate vice president for international services, emphasized the importance of getting the basics right. IU has taken a strong data-driven approach to do so. "We started from bare bones," Viers said. "What is it that we need to know, and why? What do we need to be able to track?" The result was a state-of-the-art software solution, sunapsis, which provides the institution with rich information about where its international students are coming from and how well they are performing academically at the institution. Coupled with international student satisfaction data from IU's annual participation in the International Student Barometer (ISB) survey, sunapsis enables the university to track students on a record-by-record basis to identify major trends and issues. The university incorporates information gathered from sunapsis and the ISB into a rolling yearly strategic planning process. "We are trying to do as much as we can to ensure that our practices are evidence-based," Viers continued. "What information do we need in order to make those determinations?" Sunapsis not only has proactive alerts that help students and staff manage immigration compliance issues and deadlines (e.g., students begin getting alerts six months before their passport expires), it also links with institutional data so that international recruiters and admissions advisers can ensure that students arrive on campus prepared for success. And student satisfaction data from ISB provide key information for not only the international office, but also each of IU's academic and service units. As a result of this data-driven, evidence-based approach, IU has seen gains in international students' grade point average (GPA), satisfaction, and persistence.

Too often, institutions collect reams of data that end up being stored on hard drives and campus servers or gathering dust as institutional reports. The key to IU's success has been getting the basics right, then engaging and collaborating with campus colleagues about the meaning of the data. Cross-campus dialogue is purposeful: it focuses on student success, drives action in response to trends in the data, and generates trust among key units involved in serving IU's international students. Most important, dialogue about data connects existing capacities on campus rather than leaving the international office to do everything itself. Viers emphasized this approach of connecting existing capacities on campus—identifying staff, units, faculty, and other initiatives whose efforts bolster his office's change efforts:

> Relationships, relationships, relationships. It's critical to reach out to your colleagues around campus and build relationships. One of the things we try to do in this office is to help our colleagues be as excellent as they possibly can in terms of the services that they provide to international students. We begin by striving to support them in their work and meeting their needs from us with excellence.

By sharing data from the ISB and sunapsis, the international office is able to use an evidence-based approach to respond to the needs of other units that serve international students (e.g., academic advising). As Valencia College did in the chapter 4 case example, IU has partnered with existing initiatives to enhance responsiveness to international student needs and concerns. For example, this coordinated data-driven system allows the university to schedule advising appointments early on in orientation, giving specialized advisers the information they need about students, including what placement tests they need and what issues need to be addressed early on in the advising appointment. Getting the basics right early, by sharing data and information, allows the university to proactively address issues that enhance student academic performance and increase retention.

The key to success at IU has been building long-term, trusting relationships that allow the international office to leverage existing opportunities and services. Cross-campus collaboration sometimes means reaching out to colleagues in career services, academic advising, or faculty development. According to Viers,

> I think sometimes international offices try to do too much and, in a way, sometimes the concerns we have about international students being segregated on our campuses, the international office becomes positioned in a similar way because they are not well integrated with the other units. They are trying to do it all; trying to meet every need of the student and not relying on their colleagues for what they can contribute and where their areas of expertise are.

There is hardly anything an international office does that does not have some impact on another unit. Getting the basics right—collecting and communicating data with key stakeholders—may seem simple enough. However, this approach has allowed IU to think and act systemically in ways that weren't possible before. IU's proactive, data-driven, evidence-based system can now serve as a backbone to helping ensure that the university's international students achieve success.

Neo-Racism on the Internet

Despite the social connections that new technologies afford, the Internet is by no means a neutral space that international students alone inhabit. Contrary to the idea that the Internet's virtual worlds allow international students to retreat into the comfort of intimate family and cultural networks, the Internet can also become a transparent and painful reminder of the racist, ethnocentric attitudes possessed by certain U.S. peers. Jenny Lee, an associate professor at the University of Arizona, has coined the term *neo-racism* to describe discriminatory attitudes or behavior based on one's country of origin or culture rather than skin color alone (Lee & Rice, 2007). One does not have to search far, for instance, to discover examples of the rampant racism that a good number of international students encounter via the Internet and social media. The comments section following an MSN Money article titled "America Beckons Foreign Students More Than Ever" is but one example of the racist impulse that one may find in the United States when talk turns to the issue of international students and their growing numbers at U.S. universities today (Kennedy, 2013). A commentator named shawn3179 responded to the article as follows:

> If we allow them to come here they must understand this is American [*sic*]! Our culture our customs, Merry Christmas! If you are offended to [*sic*] bad, Leave! No foot washing inside buildings if it is a christian [*sic*] school there will be Christian art and effects, if you do not like it do not come!! Our leaders and the laws must be changed to allow American culture to stay as it is and not be changed just because some Musluim [*sic*] is offended! If they stay to earn a masters or PHD and teach in lue [*sic*] of payment then they must speak "clear" English!! The only way they stay after there [*sic*] visa runs out is to have something to contribute to OUR culture of business. (shawn3179, 2013)

It might be tempting to believe that such an offensive comment represents an outlier in an otherwise tolerant American society. However, recent cases suggest otherwise. One example is an editorial titled "Public Universities Should Not Accept Students From Countries That Have Bad Relations With U.S.," published by the student newspaper at Kansas State University (KSU). This controversial op-ed piece in the KSU *Collegian* sparked outrage among international students from Afghanistan, Iran, Iraq, Turkey, and China who initiated a movement via social media to discourage fellow students from attending the university. The university quickly launched a public relations offensive to counter the negative publicity generated by this article, highlighting evidence of KSU's initiatives to ensure an atmosphere that welcomed international students and emphasizing the American tradition of free speech in such op-ed pieces. The student body president emphasized that "international students, faculty and staff provide an integral component to our student body and our university" and are "welcome and important members of our campus family" (Spriggs, 2012, para. 6). The backlash that followed this editorial highlights the complex roles that race, nationality, and prejudice play in both real-world and virtual environments.

Similarly, Princeton University faced a backlash in 2007, when it published a satire of a Chinese American student, Jian Li, who claimed his rejection at Princeton was a result of his ethnicity and who subsequently enrolled at Yale University. In the *Daily Princetonian* annual "joke issue," "Lian Ji" argues, "I mean, I love Yale. Lots of Bulldogs here for me to eat" (see also Ruble & Zhang, 2013). In 2006, an editorial in the *UCLA Daily Bruin* sarcastically proposed that to counter the "Asian invasion," the University of California (UC) system should create a new campus, "UC Merced Pandas," and funnel all "young Maos and Kim Jongs" there. The outright satire and ridicule of Asian international students in both of these cases demonstrates the neo-racism that many international students are forced to face as they pursue a U.S. education, even at some of the country's finest institutions (Lee & Rice, 2007).

Conclusion

The growth of media and communication technologies, the prevalence of social media, and the low cost and accessibility of long-distance travel allow today's international students to stay connected with faraway family and friends like never before (Elliot & Urry, 2010; Ye, 2006). The aim of this chapter has been to highlight how these virtual relationships with family and kinship networks far away foster a keen sense of belonging that transcends, and even transforms, university boundaries. Moreover, it has been shown that networks of kinship relationships mitigate many of the risks that international students confront offline. It appears that "spreading the risk" across these networks allows international students to remain resilient in ways that defy current notions regarding the negative effects of acculturative and personal stress on international student success (Lin et al., 2011; Smith & Khawaja, 2011). In addition, the use of new interactive technologies, such as the system developed at IU reviewed in this chapter, illustrates how technology also enables universities to work proactively to support and promote the success of their international students.

Although these new technologies are clearly empowering for international students and universities alike, acts of racial discrimination on campus and in online environments serve as a real and painful reminder of some of the obstacles that international students still face as they pursue a U.S. university degree in the new millennium. In the next chapter, we therefore revisit one of the core themes of this book: the importance of enhancing international students' sense of belonging in order to better ensure their success—and the success of the host institutions entrusted with educating them.

References

Anderson, K. (2013). *Anthropology, globalization, and higher education* (Unpublished master's thesis). University of Wisconsin–Madison, Madison, WI.

Birnbaum, M., & Gonzalez, M. (2012). Strangers in a strange land: How nontraditional international adult students see a United States university. *Journal of International Education and Leadership, 2*(2), 1–16.

Chickering, A. W., & Kytle, J. (1999). The collegiate ideal in the twenty-first century. *New Directions for Higher Education, 105,* 109–120.

De Verthelyi, R. F. (1995). International students' spouses: Invisible sojourners in the culture shock literature. *International Journal of Intercultural Relations, 19*(3), 387–411.

Elliot, A., & Urry, J. (2010). *Mobile lives.* New York, NY: Routledge.

Fong, V. L. (2011). The floating life: Dilemmas of education, work, and marriage abroad. In *Paradise redefined: Transnational Chinese students and the quest for flexible citizenship in the developed world.* Stanford, CA: Stanford University Press.

Gargano, T. (2009). (Re)conceptualizing international student mobility: The potential of transnational social fields. *Journal of Studies in International Education, 13*(3), 331–346. doi:10.1177/1028315308322060

Hamberger, K., Houseman, M., & White, D. R. (2011). Kinship network analysis. In J. Scott & P. J. Carrington (Eds.), *SAGE Handbook of Social Network Analysis* (pp. 533–549). Thousand Oaks, CA: SAGE Publications.

Kennedy, B. (2013, June 12). America beckons foreign students more than ever. *MSN Money.* Retrieved from http://money.msn.com/now/post.aspx?post=515e691d -eb98-4e8e-852a-d75061b45790

Lee, J. J., & Rice, C. (2007). Welcome to America? International student perceptions of discrimination. *Higher Education, 53*(3), 381–409. doi:10.1007/ s10734-005-4508-3

Lin, J.-H., Peng, W., Kim, M., Kim, S. Y., & LaRose, R. (2011). Social networking and adjustments among international students. *New Media & Society, 14*(3), 421–440. doi:10.1177/1461444811418627

Murphy, M. (2008). Variations in kinship networks across geographic and social space. *Population and Development Review, 34*(1), 19–49.

Pimpa, N. (2005). A family affair: The effect of family on Thai students' choices of international education. *Higher Education, 49*(4), 431–448. doi:10.1007/ S10734-004-2825-6

Poyrazli, S., & Kavanaugh, P. R. (2006). Marital status, ethnicity, academic achievement, and adjustment strains: The case of graduate international students. *College Student Journal, 40*(4), 767–780.

Rainie, L., & Wellman, B. (2012). *Networked: The new social operating system.* Boston, MA: MIT Press.

Ruble, R. A., & Zhang, Y. B. (2013). Stereotypes of Chinese international students held by Americans. *International Journal of Intercultural Relations, 37*(2), 202–211. doi:10.1016/j.ijintrel.2012.12.004

shawn3179. (2013, June 12). Re: America beckons foreign students more than ever [Web log comment]. Retrieved from http://money.msn.com/investing/investing-news.aspx?post=515e691d-eb98-4e8e-852a-d75061b45790

Smith, R. A., & Khawaja, N. G. (2011). A review of the acculturation experiences of international students. *International Journal of Intercultural Relations, 35*(6), 699–713. doi:10.1016/j.ijintrel.2011.08.004

Spriggs, N. (2012, March 1). Student government response to opinion piece on international students. *K-State Today*. Retrieved from http://www.k-state.edu/today/announcement.php?id=2523

Suarez-Orozco, M., Darbes, T., Dias, S. I., & Sutin, M. (2011). Migrations and schooling. *Annual Review of Anthropology, 40*, 311–328. doi:10.1146/annurev-anthro-111009-115928

Teshome, Y., & Osei-Kofi, N. (2011). Critical issues in international education: Narratives of spouses of international students. *Journal of Studies in International Education, 16*(1), 62–74. doi:10.1177/1028315311403486

Yan, K., & Berliner, D. C. (2011). An examination of individual level factors in stress and coping processes: Perspectives of Chinese international students in the United States. *Journal of College Student Development, 52*(5), 523–542. doi:10.1353/csd.2011.0060

Ye, J. (2006). Traditional and online support networks in the cross-cultural adaptation of Chinese international students in the United States. *Journal of Computer-Mediated Communication, 11*(3), 863–876. doi:10.1111/j.1083–6101.2006.00039.x

5

CAMPUS CONTEXTS THAT FOSTER A SENSE OF BELONGING

A solitary human being is literally an impossibility. You come into being because literally a community of two persons happened. I would not be able to know how to speak as a human being. I would not know how to walk as a human being. I have to learn it from other human beings, so I depend actually, completely on other human beings in order for me to be human. So the truth, yes, the truth of who we are is, "We are because we belong."

—Desmond Tutu quoted in Abbott and Shadyac (2010)

Terrell Strayhorn (2012), in his book *College Students' Sense of Belonging: The Key to Educational Success for All Students*, argues that a student's sense of belonging takes on greater importance at particular times and among certain populations. Belonging assumes greater importance, for example, in social contexts in which individuals are more likely to experience isolation or loneliness or to feel invisible as they reconstruct support networks in a new cultural and linguistic environment (Sawir, Marginson, Deumert, Nyland, & Ramia, 2007). College campuses are one such social context, then. Subway stations, in contrast, are not. With the aid of an extensive literature review on the sense of belonging among Latino students, gay students, and students of color in the science, technology, engineering, and mathematics (STEM) fields, Strayhorn demonstrates that belonging becomes a key, if not *the*, resource individuals turn to when they are in places that are unfamiliar to them and they feel marginalized.

In his book, Strayhorn notes that college students' social identities (i.e., a person's race or ethnicity, religion, gender, sexual orientation, and socioeconomic class) intersect. Indeed, the powerful interplay of multiple factors—the challenge of diasporic selfhood—when globally mobile students attempt to define their identities clearly complicates any sense of belonging, resulting for many in a sense of belonging "nowhere and everywhere" at the same time. Strayhorn shares the story of an Asian gay male student who told the author:

> Every part of me really shapes how I feel about belonging here in college. It is not my Asian side saying "yes I think here because I am smart in science," while the immigrant or working-class side of me says "you are alone here, so go home." . . . It is actually all of them at once saying a combination of both things, I guess. (Strayhorn, 2012, p. 22)

The powerful effect of belonging on social and educational outcomes provides a distinctive vantage point from which to understand international students both as individuals and as members of groups. This effect may also motivate administrators to work more actively to foster meaningful group memberships for international students at their institutions. If those of us working at U.S. institutions of higher learning continue to turn a blind eye to the fundamental role that belonging plays in human life, we cannot hope to understand the international students who come to us or the worlds that they do or may inhabit.

Enlarging Our View of International Students' Sense of Belonging

Using the case examples in this book, findings from the GPI, and our conversations with international students, we suggest three subtle but important ways that international educators and administrators might enlarge our approach to the issue of belonging when it comes to the international student population at U.S. colleges and universities. In what follows, we discuss how belonging contributes to the educational persistence and success of international students and highlight three dimensions of belonging that are critical to strengthening and deepening the international student experience of belonging at U.S. campuses today.

To begin, we advocate for a shift away from the current focus on the vulnerabilities of international students toward a more holistic, and we would argue, more constructive, focus on their resilience and strength. We subsequently discuss the need to shift from the current focus on international students as relatively unconnected, autonomous individuals to a focus on international students as participants in complex, influential, and often vast transnational social networks. Finally, we argue that international educators and administrators need to shift away from a traditional focus on professionalized student services for international students toward a focus on civic agency—the individual and collective capacity for international students to advocate for their interests.

Belonging and Resilience

A focus on belonging becomes critical once international educators and administrators decide to assume a strengths-based approach to their international students. In contrast to a vulnerabilities approach, a strengths-based approach emphasizes the individual and group resilience of international students on campus. Over the years, we have collected various headlines dealing with international students' experiences from news sources ranging from college newspapers to the *New York Times*. The headlines almost always include terms such as *struggles, challenges, pressures, stress, vulnerability, obstacles, barriers, hardships, problems*, and *need help*. Although well intentioned, headlines like "Poor, Isolated, and Far From Home: What It's Like to Be an International Student" (Paudel, 2013) may actually undermine a fuller understanding of the international student experience. In an article analyzing the stories and first-person accounts of international students, Lee (2013) noted,

> The words "struggle," "challenging," "hard" and "pressured" were used by the students in association with the word "learn" in order to refer to the growth in both personal and academic terms that they experienced as they grappled with the challenge of negotiating and constructing meaning in their respective disciplines. These examples of international students' personal journeys through the U.S. higher education system indicate not only their vulnerability, but, just as important, their endurance, adaptability, and will to succeed.

As Lee points out, the students viewed the hardship that they went through as being positive and rewarding (see Pan, 2011). This is because they viewed such hardship as something that also enriched their lives, increased their resourcefulness, and prepared them to deal with new challenges.

Catherine Montgomery (2010), in *Understanding the International Student Experience*, highlights the first-person narratives of international students. She concludes that research concentrating only on the difficulties that international students face without also considering the range of capacities international students draw upon fails to capture vital parts of the larger picture of these students' lives. She notes the striking, nearly overwhelming amount of research that concentrates on international students' "need for help" (p. 32) without taking into account the student's cultural context, social networks, and personal ways of making sense of the world, all of which mediate the impact of these experiences on each individual international student.

Most studies of acculturation processes, however, focus exclusively on the negative outcomes of nonadaptive acculturation and the stressors that may cause mental health issues, including difficulties with the language, academic distress, social and cultural adjustment issues such as homesickness and lone-liness, and financial stress. Studies focused exclusively on maladaptive out-comes tend to overlook ways in which the acculturation process might in fact promote adaptation, growth, learning, and development (Chirkov, 2009; Rudmin, 2009). Stress, in addition to leading to maladaptive outcomes, may also be the impetus for significant personal growth. In and of itself, stress is not a negative condition. Thus, a paradox of acculturation is that individuals who have experienced stresses like those described previously often display significantly higher health and performance scores as compared with the gen-eral population (Rudmin, 2009).

It is important to note that a shift toward more resilience-based mod-els of understanding the lives and experiences of mobile individuals has already occurred in the field of mobility studies. In her work on international migrants, for example, Jia-Yan Pan (2011) proposes greater use of a resilience framework for acculturation as part of her argument for a paradigm shift in the field. Drawing on research in positive psychology that examines the strong linkage between a sense of meaning and psychological well-being in cancer survivors, Pan identified a similarly clear linkage between a sense of mean-ing and well-being in international migrants. She goes on to argue against an exclusive focus on risk factors and negative coping mechanisms in the study of international migrants, urging scholars to focus instead on the influence of positive coping mechanisms in understanding both adaptive and maladaptive outcomes from second culture experiences (Smith & Khawaja, 2011).

In a study of Chinese international students studying in Australia, Pan, Wong, Chan, and Joubert (2008) found that students who engaged in meaning-making processes were more likely to report positive affect despite language difficulties, difficulties in understanding slang and jokes, difficulties with coursework, and psychosocial issues such as homesickness and loneli-ness. Meaning in life, characterized by diligence, resolve, endurance of hard-ship, concentration, and humility (Wong, 1998), significantly contributed to positive affect and mediated the relationship between acculturative stress and positive emotion. In other words, an individual's ability to make sense of his or her stressful acculturative experiences proved just as important as the expe-riences themselves. Whereas a focus on mitigating risk factors works exclu-sively to eliminate these negative encounters, a focus on student resilience looks to help international students and institutions to develop the capacity to adapt to negative encounters and to adopt positive coping mechanisms so that these stressful encounters also produce learning and growth.

We would argue that international educators and administrators do international students a disservice if they turn a blind eye to the range of coping and sense-making capacities that international students in fact possess. Moreover, since few would dispute that it is next to impossible to eliminate all risk factors from the international student experience, this is an opportune moment for educators and administrators to rethink this "need for help" paradigm in their dealings with international students. Indeed, international educators and administrators would do well to adopt a more feasible, resilience-based approach that focuses on bolstering the capacity of both their organizations and their students to adapt to sudden shocks and changed circumstances, for example, academic and campus-wide initiatives. Paradoxically, continuing to focus on the "challenges" and "stress" that international students experience may contribute, albeit inadvertently, to a deficit discourse around international students that is likely to find frailty instead of strength; fragility instead of adaptability.

Belonging and Social Capital

Friendships and close relationships have shown themselves to help individuals adapt to changing life circumstances throughout the course of their lives (Hartup & Stevens, 1997). In a world connected by information and communication technologies, some of our strongest and most intimate ties may be with friends and family who are far away geographically. In the past, moving to the United States meant sacrificing strong kinship ties at home for the weaker ties of more proximate friends and acquaintants in the host country. Thanks to the spread of and the decrease in cost of wireless technologies (e-mail, cell phones, etc.) as well as the invention of a host of social media technologies (Facebook, Google+, Instagram, LinkedIn, etc.), international students today are able to sustain strong social ties to friends and family over great distances (Lin, Peng, Kim, Kim, & LaRose, 2011). The ease with which we are able to connect to others across great distances also means that international students can solicit and receive the support that they need from friends and family almost anytime and anywhere.

As a theory, social capital has a strong empirical base in the relationship between group membership and academic outcomes. Students who have access to noneconomic forms of capital, such as language proficiency, cultural knowledge, and other kinds of credentials, are able to navigate their environment with greater ease than those who lack such capital. In other words, they benefit from the social and cultural resources that have been made available to them through their social networks. When people move to contexts that are culturally distant from their homes, they have to rebuild access ways to social capital—to those resources that their social position in their home countries may have afforded.

From a social capital perspective, the responsibility of university administrators, educators, and staff is to help international students successfully forge positive connections to other individuals and groups that will provide them with the resources that these students need to be successful. Use of a social capital perspective further suggests that traditional student services approaches no longer adequately reflect the spatial-relational realities of many international students. Now more than ever, it is becoming the responsibility of student services at U.S. institutions not only to acknowledge and engage with the existing networks of social ties that international students bring with them, but also to empower these students to create new social networks (Watt & Badger, 2009). For example, rather than framing the "lack of inter-action between international and U.S. students" as a failure of individuals who need to possess greater intercultural competence, a network perspective suggests that universities might be better off helping interconnect groups on campus—and influential individuals within those groups—to create stronger linkages that connect diverse student populations.

Adopting a social capital perspective in their work would also remind international educators and administrators that a critically important outcome of college is the formation of new social relationships. If two students both receive high GPAs, yet one student receives a plum job offer owing to social relationships while another student does not, the outcomes for these students cannot be said to be equal. If two students both achieve high scores on the graduate entrance exams, but one student feels isolated and alone while the other student feels connected and participatory, the outcomes for these students cannot be said to be equal either. Christakis and Fowler (2011), in fact, argue that one's position in a social network often matters as much as, if not more than, race, class, gender, or education. Positional inequality, which occurs when a person exists on the periphery of a social network, results in unequal rights and resources. Empowering international students necessitates—if not demands—that campus leaders help networks of international students forge ties with clusters of students that exist at the core of the university's social networks.

Obviously, it is impossible to fully grasp the network of relationships that people have and the ways these relationships work, which makes it exceedingly difficult in turn to quantify an individual's social capital. However, using social capital as a lens through which to approach international students has the potential to highlight the degree to which these students have—or lack—access to the same symbolic, social, and educational resources that their American peers enjoy.

Belonging and Civic Agency

Determining the role that education plays when it comes to questions of citizenship and belonging is the final way that we explore belonging. Historically, the notion of *citizenship* has been linked to an identifiable set of rights and responsibilities that individuals possess, by virtue of either being born to a parent or parents who are citizens (*jus sanguinis*, or "right of blood") or being born within a particular territory (*jus soli*, or "right of soil") (Rhoads & Szelenyi, 2011). Traditionally, the nation-state has been central in determining a person's rights and responsibilities, whether on the grounds of *jus sanguinis* or *jus soli*. The term *citizen* in turn evokes the notion of a clear set of rights and responsibilities, such as the right to vote and the responsibilities to uphold the laws of a specific geographical location or to pay one's taxes (Boyte, 2008). The realities of globalization, however, fundamentally challenge traditional bounded notions of citizenship through mass global student mobility, global information and communication technologies, and global organizations that span multiple national borders (Rainie & Wellman, 2012). Alongside scholars such as Boyte (2008) and Soysal (1995), we too would argue that these realities call for a changed conception of citizenship that is rooted first and foremost in the notion of participation, rather than in legal representation. Yasemin Soysal, for example, advances the idea of "postnational citizenship," in which a person's rights and responsibilities are rooted in personhood: "What were previously defined as national rights become entitlements legitimized on the basis of personhood" (Soysal, 1995, p. 6).

Traditionally, undergraduate education in general, and liberal education in particular, has viewed fostering citizenship as one of its basic responsibilities. Among other things, this responsibility has traditionally included engaging students as citizens within the governance processes of the institution. Governance involves the traditions, institutions, and decision-making processes that shape the exercise of power at a university. In the case of international students, one of the questions becomes, How does the university allocate resources and make decisions, from governing dorms to preparing food to providing affordable medical insurance? International students should be, and must be, equal citizens with an equal voice. Greater political participation of international students in campus governance does not mean that complex issues will go away; it does mean that the interests of these students will not be submerged among all of the priorities that vie for resources and attention. Belonging necessitates actual participation in the decision-making processes, both large and small, at institutions. The link between belonging and citizenship emphasizes how formal, legal decision-making processes ensure social equity among different campus constituencies and that decisions serve the economic, political, and social interests of various stakeholders, including international students.

Higher education fosters the knowledge necessary for engaged citizenship, yet it also creates a context in which students can act and organize as full citizens. Approaching international students with a focus on enhancing civic agency is not just a shift in language; it is a shift in focus. To see international students as citizens, not consumers of an education, involves purposely developing the skills and capacity for them to collectively act in their own interests on values that concern them. Most new student orientations neglect the dynamics of power and politics that shape the international student experience. We believe the capacity to organize for action is a central feature of campuses if they are to strengthen and deepen their commitment to international students. Civic agency emphasizes "the navigational capacities to negotiate and transform the world around us" (Boyte, 2008, p. 11). The individual and collective capacities to act as an agent of change enable international students to navigate, advocate for, and become full cocreators of their university education. Student services quits serving students when it believes that a particular program *is* the solution, rather than a means of organizing international students to create a solution rooted in the capacity for international students to organize and act on their own behalf.

The Changing Demographics of Today's International Students

Campus contexts that foster a sense of belonging also acknowledge the changing demographics of today's international students. Although international students are frequently referred to as one student subpopulation, they are the most diverse student subpopulation on campus. The surge in enrollment has been matched with a significant diversification in the demographic makeup of the international students' academic, socioeconomic, and cultural backgrounds. International students are increasingly a "highly heterogeneous group" (Choudaha, Orosz, & Chang, 2012, p. 2). They enroll in a greater range of institutions and have differing degrees of language proficiency and academic preparedness, differing reasons and goals for studying in the United States, and differing levels of financial resources with which to fund their U.S. education. International students with greater financial resources, for example, are generally more motivated by the experiential opportunity of studying abroad, while those with more limited financial resources generally focus on the financial aid package being offered and the level of academic support available. Understanding key differences among international student applicants today has become critical for any institution that wishes to strengthen and deepen its commitment to these students and their educational and personal success in the United States.

In what follows, we will therefore highlight five divides that increasingly shape the international student experience at U.S. institutions of higher education. The five divides we highlight include the surge in undergraduate recruitment and enrollment, the increasingly varied academic preparedness of international students, the local and global tensions manifest from new patterns of global mobility, disparities in financial circumstances, and the evidence of neo-racist attitudes toward particular subpopulations of international students. We purposefully use the word *divides* because it highlights the continuing unevenness of the international student experience at U.S. universities and colleges along these five dimensions.

Education has historically been the great equalizer in U.S. society, and thinking, a way to close the gap between rich and poor, between insiders and outsiders. However, as long as university programs and activities aimed at enhancing the international student experience continue to neglect the very real social and economic differences that exist among international students when it comes to their experience of U.S. higher education, only superficial insights will result and only superficial forms of action can be taken. Failing to confront the inequalities perpetuated, but also created, by the status quo will only exacerbate social and ethnic divides, not bridge them. Any institution interested in strengthening commitments to international students must therefore face these divides head-on and wrestle with a simple but profound reality: the international student experience is in no way equal.

Accelerating Undergraduate Enrollments

New international undergraduate enrollments in the United States are quickly nearing new international graduate enrollment levels (IIE, 2013). At the same time, a handful of U.S. institutions have dramatically increased their international undergraduate enrollments. Public research universities, in particular, have taken to recruiting larger numbers of undergraduate-level students from abroad in order to leverage their potential to sustain and expand enrollments. While the presence of top faculty, research facilities, and reputation continues to drive international graduate enrollments at U.S. universities, the potential for greater revenues from self-funded undergraduate students appears to be the main driver of international student enrollments. This surge in residential undergraduate international students has had a number of intended as well as unintended consequences. Among other things, it has forced universities to rethink both their mission and their operating procedures in a wide variety of areas, ranging from faculty–student relations and academic advising to food services; from housing and student engagement activities to residential hall programming. In addition, whereas U.S. institutions of higher education traditionally relied on informal word of mouth and reputation to recruit international students, these institutions today rely increasingly on the creation of formalized plans targeting specific international student segments. In a significant shift from just a few years ago, about one-third of U.S. institutions used third-party agents to help boost international student enrollments, a practice that tends to result in the recruitment of younger students with lower high school rankings and parents with less than a college education (Zhang & Hagedorn, 2011).

Ready or Not

Universities seeking to increase international enrollments have adapted their admissions policies to reflect the changing demographics of their international student recruits. These more flexible policies admit international students with lower English proficiency test scores via pathway or bridge programs. There has also been a rise in the use of more flexible conditional admissions policies as well as growing competition among institutions for self-funded students from high-growth markets, such as Vietnam, Saudi Arabia, China, and India. Some might say that U.S. universities have experienced something akin to a race to the bottom, whereby deflationary pressures on academic standards in the push to attract ever larger numbers of self-funded students have prompted universities to undercut admissions requirements, sometimes drastically. Minimum scores on the Test of English as a Foreign Language (TOEFL) requirement for undergraduate students at some institutions start at 61 (e.g., Arizona State University, n.d.), and other institutions now admit undergraduate students with scores as low as 45 (e.g., University of Alaska–Anchorage, 2013). The number of newly admitted Saudi students has increased eightfold at U.S. universities and colleges in the last decade (IIE, 2013). Meanwhile, the average TOEFL score for Saudi undergraduates in 2012 was 60 out of a possible 120, which was significantly lower than the minimum TOEFL score of 80 required by many U.S. universities (Educational Testing Service [ETS], 2013). Traditionally, U.S. colleges have not created specialized programs for students failing to meet the basic requirements for admission. Today, however, U.S. colleges are directing a larger number of resources toward the creation of programs and support mechanisms aimed at increasing international enrollments and ensuring international student persistence. Barmak Nassirian, a former staff member at the American Association of Collegiate Registrars and Admissions Officers, recently expressed concern over this trend, arguing that it risks creating "an enormous gray zone where all kinds of practices can be justified in the name of hand-holding and in the name of 'this student will eventually get to the right place'" (Redden, 2013a, para. 7).

Local and Global Tensions

Newspaper and magazine headlines regularly highlight the tensions that arise when U.S. students see the growth of international student numbers on campus as a form of foreign occupation aimed at "taking the seats" of otherwise qualified domestic students (Lewin, 2012). The large percentage of international students at Houston Community College, for example, raised the attention of conservative blogger Judson Bryant, who maintains the Houston Public Policy website. Bryant questioned whether it was good public policy in such a constrained budget environment "to expend tens of millions of dollars in educating students from 155 countries" (Bryant, 2012). He concluded that such an expenditure was "not proportionate and consistent with the mission of a community college" (Bryant, 2012).

At the University of Wisconsin–Madison (UW), international students as a proportion of the incoming freshman class shot up from 4% in 2011 to almost 10% in 2012. Equally striking, this proportion exceeded for the first time ever the proportion of domestic minority students admitted to the university. The Faculty Senate at UW drew on findings from university admissions data in its attempts to raise concern over the sudden surge in new international enrollments at UW. In particular, UW faculty expressed concern over the 10% decline in the proportion of in-state students coupled with a 50% increase in international student enrollments during the last 10 years (Simmons, 2013).

Similarly, 18% of freshmen at the University of Washington come from abroad. "Full-freight" paying international students subsidize low-income in-state students to make up for budget shortfalls from declining state support. In three years alone, state appropriations to the University of Washington were cut in half. In-state residents, however, did not necessarily warmly welcome the sudden influx of international students. In fact, the public greeted the sudden sharp rise in foreigners with skepticism, as this comment from Farheen Siddiqui, a freshman from Renton, Washington, illustrates:

> Morally, I feel the University should accept in-state students first, then other American students, then international students. . . . When I saw all the stories about U.W. taking more international students, I thought, "Damn, I am a minority now for being in-state." (Lewin, 2012, para. 26)

A commencement address in 2013 by Vice President Joe Biden at the University of Pennsylvania also highlights the pervasive tensions in U.S. higher education between the local and global. During his speech, Biden criticized China for surpassing the U.S. economically and mocked Chinese innovation, saying, "I love to hear people tell me—now use the vernacular—'China's going to eat our lunch'" (Marble, 2013, para. 4). As it was, 1,000 Chinese students and their families attended the commencement and listened to Mr. Biden's address and likely experienced firsthand the awkward tension between local and global sympathies. Tianpu Zhang, a graduate student in the Wharton College of Business, described his reaction to Biden's speech:

> Imagine you study abroad—say in England—and then you have worked very hard for years, spent so much sweat, toil to get that degree and wake up in the morning in your academic regalia and suddenly there is this old guy standing on the podium saying, "You guys suck." (Marble, 2013, para. 2)

As these examples illustrate, the convergence of the local and global is rife with tension. The sharp rise of international students creates unprecedented opportunities for increased intercultural understanding, but it also exacerbates existing cultural divides. Such divides not only highlight important differences in the experiences of international students from various countries; they also highlight how persistent cultural attitudes exacerbate long-standing prejudices and stereotypes. Stories, like the examples just shared, highlight the uneven and unequal experiences of international students.

The Haves and Have Nots

NAFSA (2013) estimates that the economic contribution of international students to the U.S. economy now surpasses $24 billion each year. In the 2003–2004 academic year, this same figure was an estimated $13 billion (NAFSA, 2004). Increased international undergraduate student enrollments, in particular, have filled U.S. university coffers in the last 10 years. Undergraduates are primarily self-funded and require little financial aid or additional institutional resources compared with the amount of tuition they pay. Moreover, most international students are not eligible for U.S. government financial aid; about two-thirds are entirely self-funded (IIE, 2013), and many colleges charge them additional fees as international students. The allure of climbing the economic ladder with the help of a U.S. degree has drawn students from working-class families around the world, and competition for the most talented, self-funded students has accordingly intensified. Since students from Saudi Arabia and China are most likely to arrive in the United States with full funding at the undergraduate level, they have become an especially important revenue stream for U.S. universities and a favorite target for recruiters looking for well-funded potential students. In 2012, for example, more than 60% of Chinese students in the United States funded their education solely through personal resources without any institutional aid or scholarships (Zhao, 2013).

The surge in undergraduate enrollments is an economic boon to struggling higher education institutions reeling from fierce and protracted state budget cuts. Indeed, a recent survey by the *Chronicle of Higher Education* indicates that colleges and universities that enroll international students are more likely to meet their net tuition revenue and enrollment goals (Thomason, 2013). To receive their visas, international students must demonstrate that they have sufficient financial resources to cover their college education and living expenses during their study in the United States.

The United States can learn a lesson or two from countries in which international students experience the double bind of having to pay for their education out of their own pockets while also being subject to severe federal work law restrictions. A report by United Voice (2013), a union of workers in Australia's office cleaning industry, serves as a harbinger of the issues that are likely to arise when international students who are unable to pay for college study abroad. In the report, *A Dirty Business: The Exploitation of International Students in Melbourne's Office Cleaning Industry*, United Voice describes international students in Australia who are underpaid in cash, know little about their rights as workers in the country, and report abuse and intimidation by their employers. International students represent a nearly invisible work force in Melbourne's office cleaning industry, comprising over half of its employees. Although U.S. media have yet to report anything similar in this country, confidential conversations with international students suggest that the United States is not immune to this new kind of underground work force, one composed primarily of poorly funded, disenfranchised international students:

> What I did, I'm glad that my name is not going to be on this because as many international students have to basically do this so for the entire undergrad, I had to work 30 hours a week. So I had like 15 houses, and that is what I was doing 30 hours a week. I brought my vacuum in every morning. I took all undergrad classes in the afternoon. So every day I was basically—during the week—I was cleaning. I always managed to make enough money that semester to pay another semester. You cannot take it to the bank because it is cash, so what I did, I always when tuition came due, I came to register and gave them an envelope full of twenties. Once this lady, she asked me, how come you have so much cash? I did not feel obligated to explain it, so I was just quiet. (Undergraduate, female from Eastern Europe)

Racism and Safety—The West and the Rest

Scholars and practitioners have documented discrimination toward international students, with country of origin as one of the most significant factors shaping the international student experience (Jung, Hecht, & Wadsworth, 2007; Redden, 2012). Students from China, India, South Korea, and Saudi

Arabia report significantly different experiences at U.S. universities and colleges than students from Canada, Australia, and Western Europe (Glass, Buus, & Braskamp, 2013). In the United States, students from Europe, Canada, Australia, and New Zealand report little discrimination whereas students from Africa, Latin America, Asia, and the Middle East report significant discrimination (Hanassab, 2006; Lee & Rice, 2007; Rhee & Sagaria, 2004). International students from Africa may find themselves the unwitting victims of America's unresolved history of racial discrimination and ambivalence toward African Americans. For example, one African student we interviewed felt excluded by White students. In addition, she had made international friendships with students from other African countries, yet she felt her U.S. African Americans peers distanced themselves from her because she represented an African heritage they had rejected.

Students from India and China become symbols of how globalization is affecting the U.S. economy. In recent incidents, Chinese undergraduates at U.S. institutions have found their cars spray-painted with the words "Go back home" as U.S. students' attitudes toward international students have hardened and the long-standing love-hate relationship between the United States and China continues (Pew Research Center, 2013; Redden, 2012). Students from India, in turn, encounter antagonism from U.S. students who believe that Indian students earn their degrees at U.S. institutions just to return home and "take U.S. jobs." One Indian undergraduate that we interviewed shared how a tenuous conversation with a U.S. peer suddenly became a threatening group confrontation:

> It was right in my sophomore year, we had a conversation. Suddenly, a lot of people got involved, and they said that "Come on, you internationals who come here, you take our jobs and because of you, we're going jobless!" (Undergraduate, male from Southern Asia)

He urged us, as we told him about our research, to ensure his voice was heard. He implored us to make sure U.S. students understood that students from India do not come to "steal" jobs:

> They are seeing us as job snatchers or the person who is actually eating our bread. What I want you guys to do is to tell them how to compete with internationals, especially with internationals, because everybody sees as job snatcher, they are just telling we are stealing their jobs. That is not the case and most of them go back to their countries. (Undergraduate, male from Southern Asia)

Among the most worrisome trends, students from some of the top sending countries report that personal safety has become one of their greatest concerns about studying in the United States (Glass et al., 2013). Like domestic students, international students wrestle with questions of safety and security in the United States after tragic events such as the Boston Marathon bombings. Moreover, international students have expressed concerns about being scapegoated as part of a U.S. crackdown on foreign students and student visas in the wake of the terrorist attacks on September 11, 2001, and those since (Fischer, 2013; Lau, Guttenplan, & Farrer, 2013). In addition, the sometimes immense difficulties that international students face when applying for a student visa and managing the system are also cause of significant concern. Indeed, student safety concerns climbed to one of the top-five concerns in 2012, up from 17th, among a list of 19 potential international student concerns reported in 2007 (Redden, 2013c). Interestingly enough, a mere 14% of Europeans expressed concern about safety as an influential factor in their choice to study in the United States (IIE, 2011). In contrast, nearly half of South Asian and Southeast Asian students and 41% of African students surveyed mentioned personal safety as an important factor (IIE, 2011), a finding that suggests a possible link between growing neo-racism in the United States and growing personal safety concerns among certain subsets of international students (Lingzi, 2013).

Promises Made to Me

S. Bruce Thomson, a lecturer at the University of Alberta, wrote this poem to capture the divide between the promises of glossy university brochures and some international students' experiences abroad. After countless conversations with international students about their frustrations and fears, Thomson (2006) wrote the poem to capture the human costs of inadequate support and short-term thinking that does not fully consider the fundamental human need to belong.

Promises made to me
Find a better life
opportunities abound
meet new friends
start a new life.

Come to a far away land
no family, no friends
different culture, different language
it will be okay in a far away land.

You will fit right in
it might be difficult to understand at first
but you will pick it up in no time
just fit right in.

Lots of people to help you
we will meet and greet you
lots of smiling faces
everyone is there to help you.

Reality to me
Working all the hours I can
washing dishes, flipping burgers, cleaning floors putting on the smile
working all the hours to survive.

Here I have no one to lean on
I am different here
only those like me understand
here I have just me.

I don't understand
they speak so fast
the words just fly by
I don't want to fail.

To find the end
with no support
you will have to take it again they said
to find I believed all the promises made to me.

It's easy, don't you see
I can't go home with shame and disgrace
no one there will miss me
amid all the promises made to me.

Pills, rope or a gun
each with a final end
in a far away land
where promises were made to me. (p. 819–820)[1]

On the one hand, the recent influx of new international students at American colleges and universities has created unprecedented opportunities to internationalize the experience of all students, both international and domestic. For instance, U.S. students have more opportunities than ever before to engage with non-U.S. perspectives and experiences in a U.S. classroom setting. University leaders can make a difference. It is therefore critical that U.S. institutions invest more time, thought, strategy, and resources in enhancing the quality of the international student experience. First and foremost, this means strengthening campus commitments to international students. Doing so will deepen campus internationalization efforts.

On the other hand, institutions that fail to keep their promises may experience large-scale consequences that are not easily reversed. International students bear the costs of inadequate support and short-term thinking by institutions that do not develop long-term, comprehensive strategies to support international students. As Marlene Green warned after the events of September 11, 2001, the failure of U.S. educational institutions to meet the basic requirement of a safe and secure learning environment for all students would likely have a systemic impact on international student enrollments. Indeed, Green said it would be akin to "losing a forest to a fire. It happens very quickly. But winning back the market is like re-growing the forest. It takes time and effort" (as cited in Turnbull, 2004, para. 16).

Note

1. From S. Bruce Thomson, *Qualitative Inquiry* (vol. 12, no. 4), pp. 819–821, © 2006 (SAGE Publications). Reprinted by permission of SAGE Publications.

References

Abbott, J. (Producer), & Shadyac, T. (Director). (2010). *I am* [Motion picture]. USA: Paladin.

Arizona State University. (n.d.). *International admission services.* Retrieved March 1, 2014, from https://students.asu.edu/international/future/undergrad

Boyte, H. C. (2008). Against the current: Developing the civic agency of students. *Change, 40*(3), 8–15.

Bryant, J. (2012). *Houston Community College: International students and international initiatives.* Retrieved from Houston Public Policy website: http://houstonpublicpolicy.org/houston-community-college-international-students/

Chirkov, V. (2009). Summary of the criticism and of the potential ways to improve acculturation psychology. *International Journal of Intercultural Relations, 33*(2), 177–180. doi:10.1016/j.ijintrel.2009.03.005

Choudaha, R., Orosz, K., & Chang, L. (2012). *Not all international students are the same: Understanding segments, mapping behavior.* New York, NY: World Education Services.

Christakis, N. A., & Fowler, J. H. (2011). *Connected: The surprising power of our social networks and how they shape our lives.* New York, NY: Back Bay Books.

Educational Testing Service. (2013). *Test and score data summary for TOEFLiBT®* tests. Washington, DC: Author.

Fischer, K. (2013, April 23). International students increasingly ask: Is it safe to study in the U.S.? *Chronicle of Higher Education.* Retrieved from http://chronicle .com/article/International-Students-Ask-Is/138755/

Glass, C. R., Buus, S., & Braskamp, L. A. (2013). *Uneven experiences: What's missing and what matters for today's international students.* Chicago, IL: Global Perspective Institute.

Hanassab, S. (2006). Diversity, international students, and perceived discrimination: Implications for educators and counselors. *Journal of Studies in International Education, 10*(2), 157–172. doi:10.1177/1028315305283051

Hartup, W. W., & Stevens, N. (1997). Friendships and adaptation in the life course. *Psychological Bulletin, 121*(3), 355–370. doi:10.1037/0033-2909.121.3.355

Institute of International Education. (2011). *International students in the U.S.* Washington, DC: Author.

Institute of International Education. (2013). *Open Doors 2013 report on international educational exchange.* Washington, DC: Author.

Jung, E., Hecht, M. L., & Wadsworth, B. C. (2007). The role of identity in international students' psychological well-being in the United States: A model of depression level, identity gaps, discrimination, and acculturation. *International Journal of Intercultural Relations, 31*(5), 605–624. doi:10.1016/j.ijintrel.2007.04.001

Lau, J., Guttenplan, D. D., & Farrer, L. (2013, May 19). U.S. campuses wrestle with safety perceptions. *New York Times.* Retrieved from http://www.nytimes .com/2013/05/20/us/us-campuses-wrestle-with-safety-perceptions.html

Lee, J. J. (2013). Discussant comments in the *Perceptions and Experiences of International Students in Higher Education.* San Francisco, CA: American Educational Research Association.

Lee, J. J., & Rice, C. (2007). Welcome to America? International student perceptions of discrimination. *Higher Education, 53*(3), 381–409. doi:10.1007/s10734-005-4508-3

Lewin, T. (2012, February 4). Taking more seats on campus, foreigners also pay the freight. *New York Times.* Retrieved from http://www.nytimes.com/2012/02/05/ education/international-students-pay-top-dollar-at-us-colleges.html

Lin, J.-H., Peng, W., Kim, M., Kim, S. Y., & LaRose, R. (2011). Social networking and adjustments among international students. *New Media & Society, 14*(3), 421–440. doi:10.1177/1461444811418627

Lingzi, L. (2013, May 19). U.S. campuses wrestle with safety perceptions. *New York Times.* Retrieved from http://www.nytimes.com/2013/05/20/us/us-campuses-wrestle-with-safety-perceptions.html

Marble, W. (2013, May 22). International students concerns by Biden's commencement message. *Daily Pennsylvanian.* Retrieved from http://www.thedp.com/ article/2013/05/international-students-concerned-by-bidens-commencement -message

Montgomery, C. (2010). *Understanding the international student experience.* New York, NY: Palgrave Macmillan.

National Association of Foreign Student Advisers. (2004). *The economic benefits of international education to the United States: A statistical analysis.* Retrieved from https://www.nafsa.org/_/File/_/Washington.pdf

National Association of Foreign Student Advisers. (2013). *The economic benefits of international students to the U.S. economy.* Retrieved from http://www.nafsa.org/_/File/_/eis2013/USA.pdf

Pan, J.-Y. (2011). A resilience-based and meaning-oriented model of acculturation: A sample of mainland Chinese postgraduate students in Hong Kong. *International Journal of Intercultural Relations, 35*(5), 592–603. doi:10.1016/j.ijintrel.2011.02.009

Pan, J.-Y., Wong, D. F. K., Chan, C. L. W., & Joubert, L. (2008). Meaning of life as a protective factor of positive affect in acculturation: A resilience framework and a cross-cultural comparison. *International Journal of Intercultural Relations, 32*(6), 505–514. doi:10.1016/j.ijintrel.2008.08.002

Paudel, S. (2013, September 12). Poor, isolated, and far from home: What it's like to be an international student. *Guardian.* Retrieved from http://www.theguardian.com/education/mortarboard/2013/sep/12/what-its-like-to-be-an-international-student

Pew Research Center. (2013). *Americans and Chinese grow more wary of each other.* Washington, DC: Author.

Rainie, L., & Wellman, B. (2012). *Networked: The new social operating system.* Cambridge, MA: MIT Press.

Redden, E. (2012, October 16). I'm not racist, but. *Inside Higher Ed.* Retrieved http://www.insidehighered.com/news/2012/10/16/tensions-simmer-between-american-and-international-students

Redden, E. (2013a, January 3). Conditionally yours. *Inside Higher Ed.* Retrieved January 03, 2013, from http://www.insidehighered.com/news/2013/01/03/conditional-admission-and-pathway-programs-proliferate

Redden, E. (2013c, June 27). Paying a premium. *Inside Higher Ed.* Retrieved from http://www.insidehighered.com/news/2013/06/27/canadian-university-questions-about-engineering-program-enrolling-almost-exclusively

Rhee, J., & Sagaria, M. A. D. (2004). International students: Constructions of imperialism in the *Chronicle of Higher Education. Review of Higher Education, 28*(1), 77–96. doi:10.1353/rhe.2004.0031

Rhoads, R. A., & Szelenyi, K. (2011). *Global citizenship and the university: Advancing social life and relations in an interdependent world.* Stanford, CA: Stanford University Press.

Rudmin, F. (2009). Constructs, measurements and models of acculturation and acculturative stress. *International Journal of Intercultural Relations, 33*(2), 106–123. doi:10.1016/j.ijintrel.2008.12.001

Sawir, E., Marginson, S., Deumert, A., Nyland, C., & Ramia, G. (2007). Loneliness and international students: An Australian study. *Journal of Studies in International Education, 12*(2), 148–180. doi:10.1177/1028315307299699

Simmons, D. (2013, May 9). Wisconsin students decline, international students rise as percentage of most recent UW–Madison freshman class. *Wisconsin State Journal.* Retrieved from http://host.madison.com/news/local/education/university/wisconsin-students-decline-international-students-rise-as-percentage-of-most/article_cb3e6538-2abe-5207-8aa8-a19d8145a26f.html

Smith, R. A., & Khawaja, N. G. (2011). A review of the acculturation experiences of international students. *International Journal of Intercultural Relations, 35*(6), 699–713. doi:10.1016/j.ijintrel.2011.08.004

Soysal, Y. N. (1995). *Limits of citizenship: Migrants and postnational membership in Europe.* Chicago, IL: University of Chicago Press.

Strayhorn, T. L. (2012). *College students' sense of belonging: A key to educational success for all students.* New York, NY: Routledge.

Thomason, B. A. (2013, October 15). Diversity aside, international students bring a financial incentive. *Chronicle of Higher Education.* Retrieved from http://chronicle.com/blogs/bottomline/diversity-aside-international-students-bring-a-financial-incentive/

Thomson, S. B. (2006). Promises made to me. *Qualitative Inquiry, 12*(4), 819–821. doi:10.1177/1077800406288625

Turnbull, L. (2004, November 15). Fewer students from abroad. *Seattle Times.* Retrieved from http://seattletimes.com/html/localnews/2002091104_intlstudent15m.html

United Voice. (2013). *A dirty business: The exploitation of international students in Melbourne's office cleaning industry.* Melbourne: Author.

University of Alaska–Anchorage. (2013, December 10). *Admission requirements.* Retrieved from http://www.uaa.alaska.edu/international-student-services/new-student/apply.cfm

Watt, S. E., & Badger, A. J. (2009). Effects of social belonging on homesickness: An application of the belongingness hypothesis. *Personality and Social Psychology Bulletin, 35*(4), 516–30. doi:10.1177/0146167208329695

Wong, P. (1998). *Personal meaning profile.* Retrieved from http://www.drpaulwong.com/documents/wong-scales/personal-meaning-profile.pdf

Zhang, Y., & Hagedorn, L. S. (2011). College application with or without assistance of an education agent. *Journal of College Admission, 67*(2), 6–16.

Zhao, E. (2013, March 27). Chinese students struggle for returns on education in U.S. [Web log post]. *China Realtime.* Retrieved from http://blogs.wsj.com/chinarealtime/2013/03/27/chinese-students-struggle-for-returns-on-education-in-u-s/

6

RECOMMENDATIONS FOR PRACTICE

The aim of this book has been to explore some of the actions that universities and colleges across the United States have taken to create more inclusive, connected, and purposeful campus environments for their international students. As part of this exploration, we have placed particular emphasis on the importance of tapping and reinforcing each institution's existing strengths and capacities in the development of strategies that will enable it to create more inclusive campus climates for current and incoming international students.

Moreover, we firmly believe that any college or university wishing to strengthen its campus commitment to international students must reach out and engage in active collaboration with all departments and offices across the campus, with the larger community, and most important, with the international student community itself.

Finally, although the colleges and universities we highlight in this book are very different from one another, the international programs, policies, and practices that they have implemented nonetheless evolved from a shared basic insight. Because the demographics of today's international students have shifted and expanded, so too must the university programs, policies, and practices designed to meet their present educational, professional, and social needs. Accordingly, the final chapter of this book offers recommendations for universities and colleges committed to adjusting and realigning their institutions to enhance the international student experience in an age of mass student global mobility.

In what follows, we briefly revisit some of the key features of the initiatives highlighted in the book and make recommendations that we believe will help create more positive campus environments for international students today. We prefer to characterize these efforts to enhance the international student experience in terms of strengthening, deepening, and expanding commitments to international students rather than using the language of change or reform. This language reflects, again, the importance of building on what is already there, including strengthening connections among various units, exploring ways to deepen the quality of the international student experience, and expanding the number of all students engaged in international, global, and intercultural learning.

Helping International Students Thrive: Recommendations for Practice

Succeeding as an international educator means making a difference in students' lives—helping international students to thrive at their host university. At the same time, international educators often find themselves leading from the middle; advancing change while working with cross-campus colleagues; responding to visions of the president, provost, and vice president; and managing a diverse network of students and programs. Those of us who lead from the middle do not set, or often have any significant influence over, the strategic focus areas of the entire institution. Therefore, enacting change requires coordination across a vast and complex array of units (academic advising, housing and residence life, etc.), each of which is also advancing its own priorities and goals.

Authority and decision making are distributed across so many different units that higher education institutions have been aptly characterized as "organized anarchies" (Cohen & March, 2000, p. 195). These unique organizational dynamics necessitate a particular stance toward leadership and organizational change designed to enhance the international student experience (Heyl, Thullen, & Brownell, 2007). Although a university's strategic plan might neatly outline four or five major priorities, more realistically, hundreds of competing priorities vie for senior leaders' attention. Consequently, international students' concerns may be overlooked, suppressed, or get discussed but not vigorously acted upon. Navigating this complex organizational environment often frustrates mid-level international educators seeking to strengthen their campus's commitment to international students.

While mid-level administrators who work directly with international students are responsible for informing senior administrators about programs, resources, and outcomes, many have little influence over the university's major strategic and budgetary priorities. Moreover, at many institutions, resources allocated to the international student programs and services may be limited, and international programs and services may receive little attention beyond a small subset of campus administrators, faculty, and students. To meet this challenge, effective mid-level international educators must understand where and how the international student community fits in with the institution's strategic goals, agenda, and profile. Using the case examples in this book, we offer the following recommendations:

- Connect international initiatives with the institution's existing strategic priorities
- Focus on continuous, data-driven approaches to decision making
- Forge flexible coalitions with key campus stakeholders

Connect International Initiatives With the Institution's Existing Strategic Priorities

While U.S. institutions have made significant progress in implementing comprehensive internationalization, it is still not an expressed priority at many colleges and universities (American Council on Education, 2012). If you are fortunate enough to be at an institution that has seen a significant expansion in resources designated to support international students—not just increasing international enrollments—as one of its top priorities, then please feel free to skip this section. Realistically, however, many international educators face increasing international student enrollments with stagnant or, at best, modest increases in the resources necessary to support meaningful and effective international student programming and services.

Given this state of affairs, international educators must articulate their goals in language that reflects and builds on the institution's strategic priorities. Connecting international programming and services to existing strategic priorities is far more effective, in our opinion, than vying to get to the top of the institutional agenda with programs and services that don't speak to the strategic priorities already in place.

Connect international initiatives to existing efforts for student engagement and success. In practical terms, we recommend that mid-level international educators identify strategic goals for their unit and then translate those goals into the language of existing institutional priorities, emphasizing, as a whole, how their offices are essential to the success of these broader initiatives for student engagement and success. For example, student engagement and success are top priorities at a growing number of institutions, and the notion that campus internationalization enhances student learning is often championed. At the same time, international student initiatives may not be framed in terms of how they enhance the institution's broader goals for student learning, including student success, retention, and achievement of essential learning outcomes. Often, these connections go unstated because they seem clear to international educators involved in day-to-day interactions with international students. However, forging a clear connection between international student initiatives and an institution's strategic priorities helps senior administrators, too, to see these connections more clearly. For instance, in the case example from Florida International University, international educators connected the existing activities of their office with the institution's QEP process. As another example, the I-House at Northern Arizona University (NAU) linked its efforts at increasing international student recruitment with NAU's strategic focus on its GSEP. International educators at both FIU and NAU thus focused on framing their initiatives in obvious line with the existing strategic language and goals of their respective institutions to enhance international student learning.

Invest in faculty learning and professional growth. All of the institutions that we examined explored ways to deepen the quality of the international student experience in the classroom and on campus. As the campus example from Valparaiso University illustrates, fostering a culture of learning requires that professors develop an in-depth understanding of the cultural and ethnic backgrounds of the international students they teach and advise. Often, university administrators focus on efforts designed to help international students adapt to a U.S.-style classroom. We believe, however, that institutions must place an equally strong focus on helping faculty to adapt their teaching styles and develop their cultural sensitivities toward non-U.S. students. Often, international students arrive in the U.S. classroom possessing a culturally different approach to the classroom and to learning. Purposeful faculty development, in this case, might include international travel to the home countries of the international students that professors are responsible for teaching. "Faculty field trips" of this kind would help faculty to develop sensitivities that they may not have had before and to fine-tune their pedagogical approaches to the needs of a more globally diverse student population. When travel is not possible, international educators can purposefully use existing programs to connect international students with faculty members outside the classroom. Examples of such initiatives range from weekly international coffee hours, mini presentations hosted by international educators or international students, and faculty member participation in large-scale international student cultural events. Just as international educators strive to create powerful international, global, and intercultural learning opportunities for students, so too should they strive to provide similarly powerful learning opportunities for faculty.

Expand existing initiatives that are already purposeful and effective. The success of the institutional initiatives examined in the book did not necessarily come from their newness. Instead, their success came from the ways in which these initiatives successfully piggybacked on the momentum of existing resources and activities. Elon University, for example, did not reinvent the wheel in the case of Study USA. Instead, it saw an opportunity to engage international students too in an already fully operational study away program. This initiative thus scaled up a practice already known for its purposefulness and effectiveness, significantly expanding the number of students able to benefit from it.

Focus on Continuous, Data-Driven Approaches to Decision Making

Higher education institutions are notorious for collecting reams and reams of assessment data. Assessment data provide administrators with the evidence they need to evaluate activities, programs, and services. In our experience, however, the political dimension of assessment is also critical to acknowledge: campus units want to report good news to justify their programs and activities. This results, then, in a strong emphasis on those data that support a positive narrative (e.g., There is significant growth in international enrollments) and a clear deemphasis of the data that support a negative narrative (e.g., There is evidence that international students feel disconnected from or discriminated against by U.S. peers). When assessment data are used to evaluate and improve the experience of international students at U.S. universities, we suggest that international educators and administrators follow four essential principles:

Do not treat international students as one group in institutional assessment. We believe that institutions should include variables and indicators such as country of origin, sources of financial aid, and levels of academic preparedness (Choudaha, Orosz, & Chang, 2012). As campuses enroll more demographically diverse international student populations, it is important to disaggregate the data to see whether international students' experiences and outcomes are uneven (Glass, Buus, & Braskamp, 2013). For example, although pathway programs promise equivalent learning outcomes at the end of a bachelor's degree, little research on whether students who enroll in pathway programs actually exhibit equivalent learning outcomes as compared with their more academically prepared counterparts has been undertaken. Moreover, despite evidence that the experiences of international students may vary substantially according to the student's country of origin, data on international students are rarely disaggregated by this variable.

Focus on connecting the data already collected, not on collecting more data. Often, an enhanced assessment of the international student experience at an institution does not necessitate the launch of a completely new set of institutional research studies. Instead, what is frequently required is an effort to connect the data that have already been collected. For example, institutions can look at the NSSE, the ISB, the GPI, demographic data from international student services, and other existing institutional data on student learning and success. Indiana University, for instance, tracks how students recruited through specific channels perform academically (e.g., students from specific international high schools, specific partnership arrangements). Integrating and culling valuable information from existing data sets thus allows institutions to realign international student initiatives and programs more quickly and efficiently so as to ensure that they are meeting the real needs of these students and enhancing their academic success.

Put someone in charge of sharing key findings with stakeholders. Even in the age of technology, it takes a person to connect the dots across data sets and to engage key stakeholders in a discussion about how these now-connected dots reveal important trends and results. Dialogue about data thus requires international educators to proactively invite themselves to meetings of key stakeholder groups to share what they are learning from assessment data. Open discussions about the meaning of data in turn invite stakeholders to play a key role too in interpreting the meaning of trends and identifying potential actions to address issues raised through the discussion. Such purposeful discussions may result in more effective coordination between units, greater awareness about troubling trends and issues, and the formation of relationships more generally that facilitate greater communication and coordination across all units.

Tell the story as you provide the proof. Although assessment often involves quantitative survey data, ensuing discussions with key stakeholders routinely entail stories that illustrate the issues and trends indicated by the data. We believe that the stories that surface in the course of such discussions can be as potent as the data themselves and that international educators should weave these stories into their meetings with senior administrators to help administrators grasp more vicariously the nature and significance of the key trends being discussed.

Forge Flexible Coalitions With Key Campus Stakeholders

International educators work hard to ensure that international students engage, collaborate, and network with other students in a variety of ways. Often, however, international educators fail to create the same variety of sustainable collaborative networks for themselves and their respective units.

Indeed, the importance of collaboration in creating and delivering effective and sustainable international student programs and services cannot be overestimated.

Integrating international students requires integrating (or at least coordinating) various campus offices and units. International educators strive to ensure that their initiatives enhance student learning, enrich the student experience, and support student achievement. Theoretically, certainly, international educators understand that partnering is a key to success and that no single unit can act alone. At the same time, the lack of international student integration at U.S. universities and colleges has become a regular theme at recent national conferences (Fischer, 2014). Some international educators have also pointed out that there is an equally significant lack of contact and coordination between many international offices and other units on campus, a disconnect that serves to exacerbate the outsiderness of international students institutionally. All of the campuses we examined emphasized the importance of strengthening connections among various units across campus that interact with international students in different capacities. Valencia College, through its reorganization and strategic focus on international education, managed to transform its disjointed and siloed institutional structures into a fully integrated effort to enhance the international student experience. For example, through a partnership between its international and internship offices, the college helps international students engage in field experiences related to their majors. This purposeful coordination not only builds strong relationships with the surrounding community; it also provides meaningful opportunities for international students' learning and professional growth.

Partner to advocate, not just cooperate. We encourage a vision of partnership that extends beyond cross-campus cooperation to deliver more integrated services for international students. Partnership across units is also an essential political tool that can be used to advocate for change when the need arises. Partnerships are necessary when multiple offices must coordinate to give voice to issues that are critical to international student well-being and success. Strong social networks built on trust and mutual support with administrators, faculty, and student groups across campus generate social capital that international students can draw on should they need to make their voices heard on a particular issue or act in their own best interest. For example, at Old Dominion University (ODU), the ISAB relied on the social capital it had accumulated with senior faculty members and administrators in earlier collaborations to advocate for revamped health insurance requirements for all international students at the university. Indeed, the ISAB maintains regular contact with a host of important stakeholders, ranging from ODU's upper administrators and offices (e.g., the Office of the University

President, Career Management Services, and Housing and Residence Life) to key faculty advocates, the Student Government Association, and of course, the broader international student community.

Collaborating With the International Student Community

Finally, in any effort to strengthen the commitment of a campus to international students, we would argue that the single most important partner in collaboration efforts is the international student community itself. In reviewing the content of our campus case examples and interviews, we have come to understand that international educators are most influential when the changes that they seek hinge on enabling international students to organize and act on their own behalf. Strengthening campus commitments to international students is not just about what we do as international educators, but also about how we empower international students to act for themselves. The following story from one of our student interviews illustrates the enormous power of this enabling approach to change:

> I am inspired and encouraged by the mission and direction of a university that allows us to openly discuss issues pertaining to international student affairs—a university where we are given opportunities to provide our constructive feedback. I remember our focused discussions on international student interests. Together as a team, we have worked to design the most effective international programs and create the best environment for students. We want to make sure international students maintain a good opinion of this university and continue to recommend the university for their education to future international students.
>
> Engaging with the international student community enriches the quality of student life for all students. We have an opportunity to learn the internal operations of the university and appreciate the scope of various international programs through sincere conversations with the educators and administrators. Engaging the international student community is vital in building a strong student–university relationship. I would advise any university to make a consistent effort to engage the international students, and I am certain that international students will find time to engage, if given the opportunity. (Graduate, male from Southern Asia)

Conclusion

All of the institutions highlighted in this book have made substantive progress in enhancing the educational and social experience of their international students. At the same time, every institution we interviewed stressed that only focused and sustained efforts over several years would fundamentally change the relationship between their institution and an increasingly diverse international student body. Comprehensive and transformative change is certainly possible, but it rarely happens quickly. Instead, it tends to result from the accumulation of a massive number of smaller day-to-day tactical efforts carried out on the ground by international educators leading from the middle.

One of the overall aims of this book was to take the reader on a journey— from community colleges to liberal arts institutions to large public flagship research universities, from rural parts of the United States to highly populated urban areas. We hope that the case examples included in the book, findings from the GPI survey, and the accompanying international student narratives have offered the reader a complex and thought-provoking portrait of just how much U.S. university life has changed as the number and demographics of international students have changed over the last decade. We hope too that our exploration of the complexity of this portrait has helped readers to better understand the tremendous challenges that often confront senior administrators when they seek to create more inclusive, connected, and purposeful campus environments for current and prospective international students.

Strengthening the commitment of any campus to its international students undoubtedly requires the steady, determined, and preferably unanimous application of human resources, time, and money to the endeavor. As this book has attempted to show, it is the accumulation of our daily efforts, often from the middle, that will prove most likely to enable our institutions to create more inclusive, connected, and purposeful campus environments. The task is great, to be sure, but the steps can be small. We wish you the best, then, as you take the next step toward strengthening and deepening the commitment that your campus has to its international students, both those who are there and those yet to come.

References

American Council on Education. (2012). *Mapping internationalization on U.S. campuses: 2012 edition*. Washington, DC: Author.

Choudaha, R., Orosz, K., & Chang, L. (2012). *Not all international students are the same: Understanding segments, mapping behavior*. New York, NY: World Education Services.

Cohen, M., & March, J. (2000). Leadership in an organized anarchy. *Organization and Governance in Higher Education*, 195–215. doi:10.1007/978-1-4899-0885-8_4

Fischer, K. (2014, March 2). Helping foreign students thrive on U.S. campuses. *New York Times*. Retrieved from http://www.nytimes.com/2014/03/03/world/americas/helping-foreign-students-thrive-on-us-campuses.html

Glass, C. R., Buus, S., & Braskamp, L. A. (2013). *Uneven experiences: What's missing and what matters for today's international students*. Chicago, IL: Global Perspective Institute.

Heyl, J. D., Thullen, M., & Brownell, B. A. (2007). *The senior international officer (SIO) as change agent*. Washington, DC: Association of International Education Administrators.

ABOUT THE AUTHORS

Chris R. Glass is an assistant professor in the Department of Educational Foundations and Leadership at Old Dominion University (ODU), the program coordinator for ODU's Higher Education graduate program, and director of the International Higher Education Leadership track. He has been actively involved in national efforts to identify educational experiences that contribute to international students' positive development. He takes a social psychological approach to researching issues in American higher education, with an interest in how the presence of others affects educational outcomes such as achievement, motivation, and social development. He is a lead researcher on the Global Perspective Inventory (GPI), which examines the relationship between educational experiences and global learning outcomes using the survey responses of 70,000 undergraduates, including over 5,000 international students, at 135 American colleges and universities. He has published articles in the *Journal of Educational Psychology*, the *International Journal of Intercultural Relations*, the *Journal of Studies in International Education*, and *New Directions for Higher Education*. His research has also been featured in *Inside Higher Ed*. Before he came to ODU, he worked at Michigan State University in multiple administrative roles, including at the Institute for Research on Teaching and Learning, the Global Institute for Higher Education, and the National Center for the Study of University Engagement.

Rachawan Wongtrirat has a doctorate in higher education administration with a concentration in international higher education leadership. Wongtrirat is an active international educator with experience in the private and non-profit sectors and in higher education. Currently, she is the assistant director for international initiatives in the Office of Intercultural Relations at (OIR) ODU. In this role, she manages a comprehensive international unit within the OIR that supports the university's commitment to preparing its members for interaction and leadership within an interconnected global society. She researches and applies her research to practices. She has firsthand experience collaborating with international students to create an inclusive community and to implement cultural and international educational opportunities for authentic interaction and learning among the international and domestic university communities. Wongtrirat has given presentations on topics

113

related to international student recruitment and the engagement and academic achievement of international students at conferences sponsored by the National Association of Foreign Student Advisers (NAFSA) and the Comparative and International Education Society and at the Colonial Academic Alliance Global Education Conference and the EducationUSA East Asia and Pacific Regional Conference. Before she worked at ODU, Wongtrirat was an EducationUSA adviser and a program officer for Advising and Education Services at the Institute of International Education (IIE) Southeast Asia Office in Bangkok, Thailand.

Stephanie Buus's current research interests center on the influence of internationalization processes in the higher education systems of the United States and the European Union. She has participated in study abroad programs at the high school, college, graduate school, and postdoctoral levels in several countries and spent more than a decade working as an international researcher at institutes and universities in Denmark and Sweden. A graduate of the University of Michigan–Ann Arbor, Buus received her PhD in Scandinavian languages and literatures from the University of California, Berkeley, and holds an EdS from ODU. In August 2014 Stephanie relocated to Paris, France, to continue her research.

She provides the background for assessment, highlights how the characteristics of international education pose unique challenges for assessment, considers the contexts to which assessment may be applied—whether in cross-border or "at-home" institutional experiences, such as in curricular, cocurricular or extracurricular settings—and distills a seemingly convoluted process into a manageable approach.

22883 Quicksilver Drive
Sterling, VA 20166-2102   Subscribe to our e-mail alerts: www.Styluspub.com

Also available from Stylus

Building Cultural Competence
Innovative Activities and Models
Edited by Kate Berardo and Darla K. Deardorff
Foreword by Fons Trompenaars

"A new book of training activities is always welcome, but this volume offers something more: a thoughtful, careful analysis of how to design and execute relevant cultural training. You get the toolkit, in short, as well as guidance from some of the master builders."

—*Craig Sorti,*
author, trainer, and consultant in intercultural
communications

For HR directors, corporate trainers, college administrators, diversity trainers, and study abroad educators, this book provides a cutting-edge framework and an innovative collection of ready-to-use tools and activities to help build cultural competence—from the basics of understanding the core concepts of culture to the complex work of negotiating identity and resolving cultural differences.

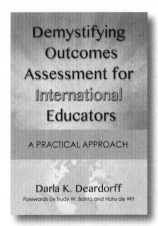

Demystifying Outcomes Assessment for International Educators
A Practical Approach
Darla K. Deardorff
Forewords by Trudy W. Banta and Hans de Wit

This book is a practical guide to learning-outcomes assessment in international education for practitioners who are starting to engage with the process, as well as for those who want to improve the quality and effectiveness of their assessment efforts.

Assuming no prior knowledge, the book offers an accessible and clear road map to the application of assessment. Recognizing that a "one-size-fits-all" approach cannot capture the diversity of goals and settings of international education, or the rich variety of programs and organizations involved in delivering it, author Darla K. Deardorff provides the reader with foundational principles and knowledge to develop appropriate assessment approaches for evaluating and improving student learning outcomes, which are the drivers of higher education internationalization.